A-Z SALISBURY

G000254516

CONTENTS

Key to Map Pages   Back Cover

Map Pages   2-41

Large

Index to Streets, Towns, Villages, Stations, Hospitals etc. and selected Places of Interest   43-52

REFERENCE

A Road	A30
B Road	B3080
Dual Carriageway	
One-way Street Traffic Flow on A Roads is also indicated by a heavy line on the driver's left.	
Road Under Construction Opening dates are correct at the time of publication.	
Proposed Road	
Restricted Access	
Pedestrianized Road	
Track & Footpath	
Residential Walkway	
Railway	Station / Tunnel / Level Crossing
Built-up Area	YORK RD.
Local Authority Boundary	
National Park Boundary	
Posttown Boundary	
Postcode Boundary (within Posttown)	
Map Continuation 10	Large Scale City Centre 42

Car Park (selected)	P
Church or Chapel	†
Cycleway (selected)	
Fire Station	■
Hospital	H
House Numbers (A & B Roads only)	78 / 25
Information Centre	i
National Grid Reference	415
Park & Ride	Wilton P+R
Police Station	▲
Post Office	★
Safety Camera with Speed Limit Fixed cameras and long term road work cameras. Symbols do not indicate camera direction.	30
Toilet: without facilities for the Disabled with facilities for the Disabled	▽ ▽
Educational Establishment	▢
Hospital or Healthcare Building	▢
Industrial Building	▢
Leisure or Recreational Facility	▢
Place of Interest	▢
Public Building	▢
Shopping Centre or Market	▢
Other Selected Buildings	▢

SCALE

Map Pages 2-41	Map Page 42
1:15,840 4 inches (10.16 cm) to 1 mile 6.31 cm to 1 km	1:7,920 8 inches (20.32 cm) to 1 mile 12.63 cm to 1 km
0 ¼ ½ Mile	0 ⅛ ¼ Mile
0 250 500 750 Metres	0 100 200 300 Metres

Copyright of Geographers' A-Z Map Company Limited

Fairfield Road, Borough Green, Sevenoaks, Kent TN15 8PP
Telephone: 01732 781000 (Enquiries & Trade Sales)
            01732 783422 (Retail Sales)
www.az.co.uk
Copyright © Geographers' A-Z Map Co. Ltd.
Edition 2 2013

 Ordnance Survey®   This product includes mapping data licensed from Ordnance Survey® with the permission of the Controller of Her Majesty's Stationery Office.
© Crown Copyright 2012. All rights reserved. Licence number 100017302
Safety camera information supplied by www.PocketGPSWorld.com
Speed Camera Location Database Copyright 2012 © PocketGPSWorld.com

Every possible care has been taken to ensure that, to the best of our knowledge, the information contained in this atlas is accurate at the date of publication. However, we cannot warrant that our work is entirely error free and whilst we would be grateful to learn of any inaccuracies, we do not accept any responsibility for loss or damage resulting from reliance on information contained in this publication.

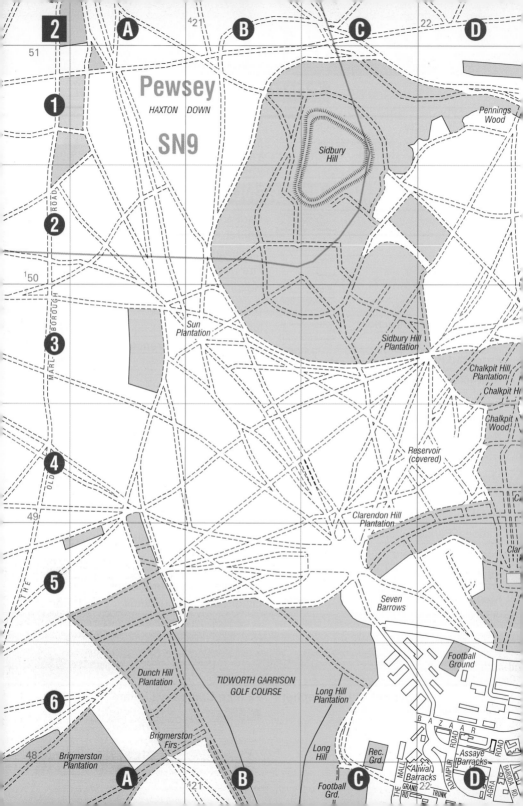

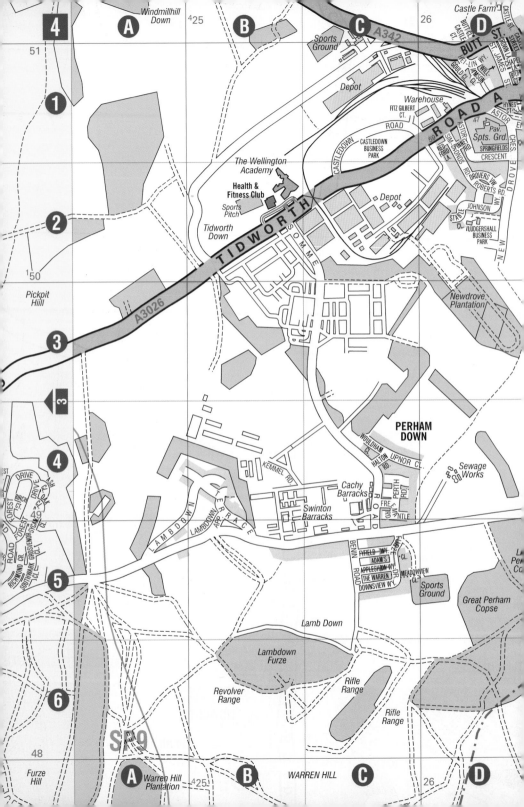

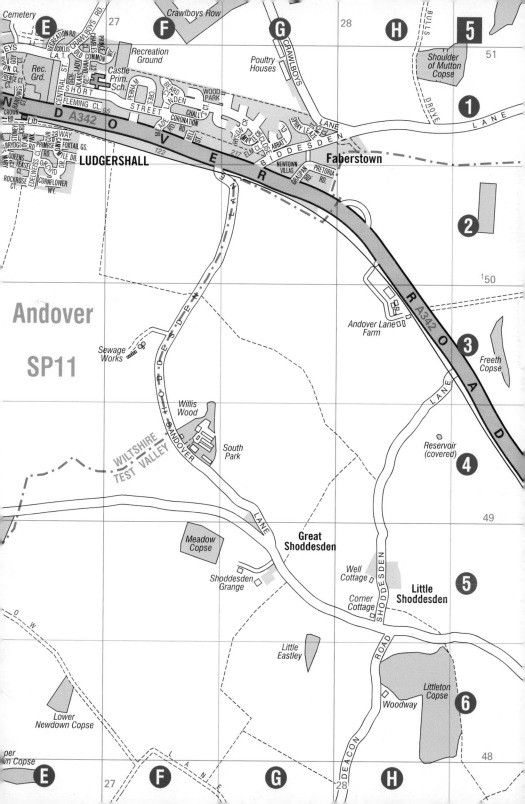

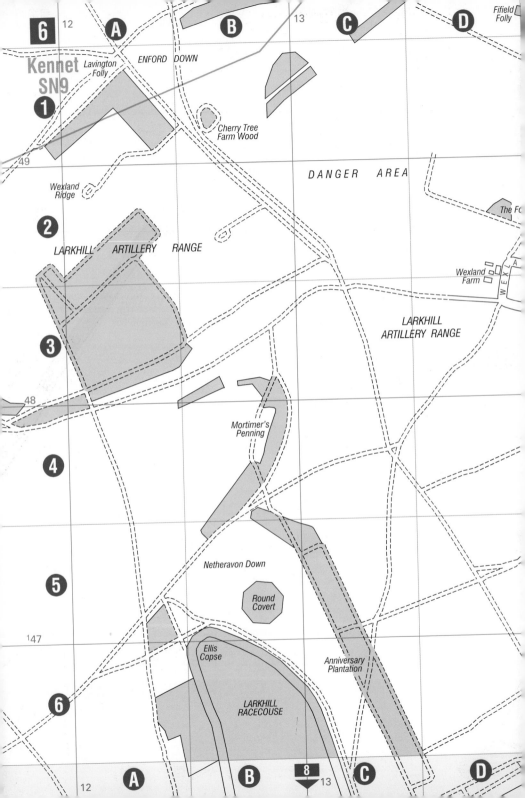

6 12 · **A** · **B** 13 · **C** · **D** Fifield Folly

Kennet
SN9 Lavington Folly · ENFORD DOWN

1

Cherry Tree Farm Wood

49

DANGER AREA

The F...

Wexland Ridge

2

LARKHILL ARTILLERY RANGE

Wexland Farm

WEXLA...

LARKHILL ARTILLERY RANGE

3

48

Mortimer's Penning

4

5

Netheravon Down

Round Covert

147

Ellis Copse

Anniversary Plantation

6

LARKHILL RACECOUSE

A 12 · **B** · **8** 13 · **C** · **D**

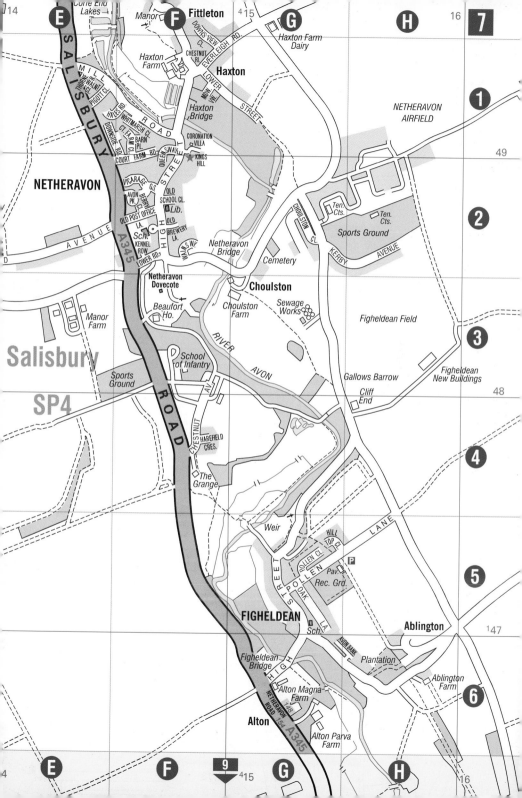

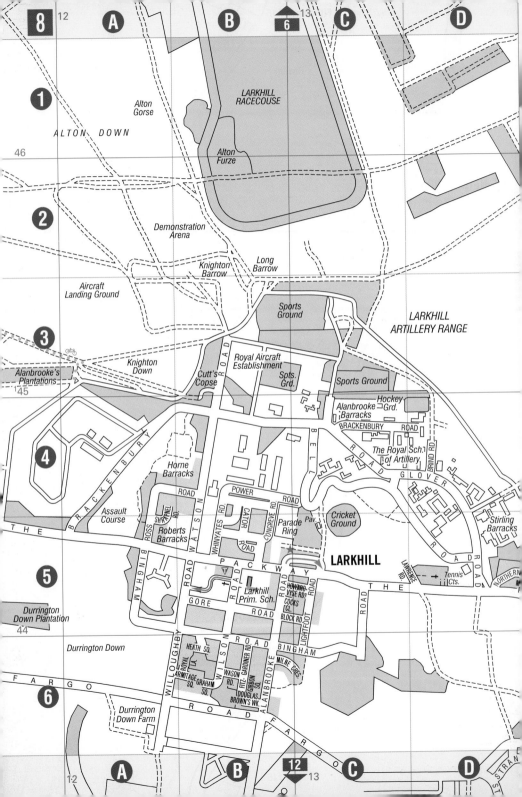

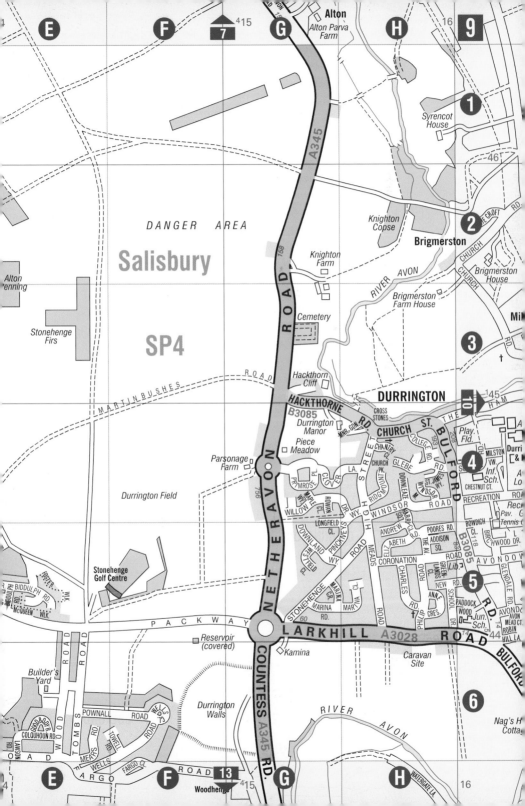

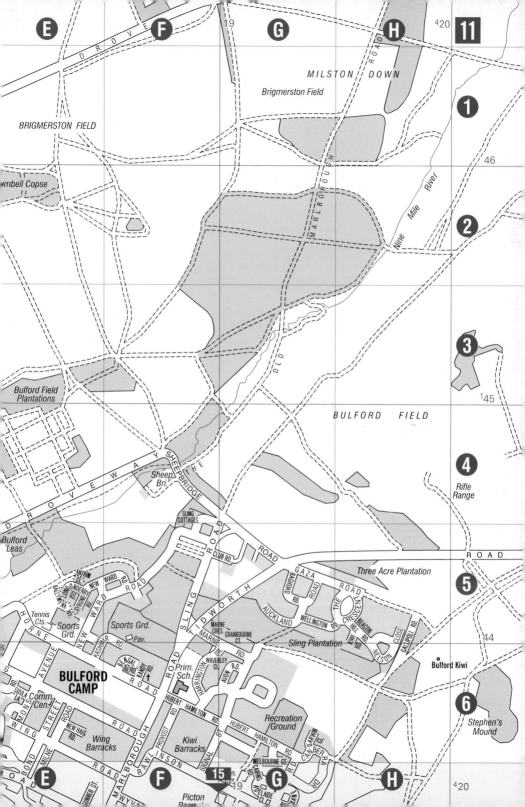

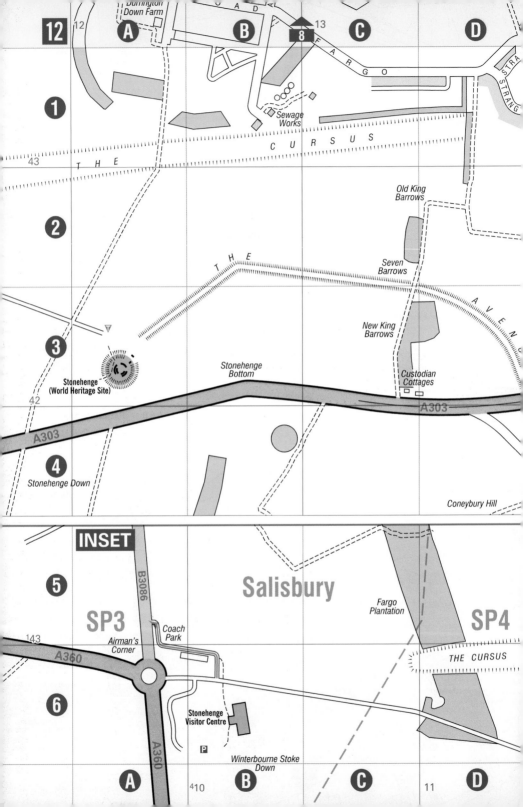

12

12 **A** **B** 13 **C** **D**

8

Durrington
Down Farm

1

Sewage
Works

C U R S U S

43 T H E

Old King
Barrows

2

T H E

Seven
Barrows

A V E N U

New King
Barrows

3

Stonehenge
(World Heritage Site)

Stonehenge
Bottom

Custodian
Cottages

42

A303

A303

4

A303

Stonehenge Down

Coneybury Hill

INSET

Salisbury

5

B3086

Fargo
Plantation

SP3

Coach
Park

SP4

143

Airman's
Corner

THE CURSUS

A360

6

Stonehenge
Visitor Centre

A360

P

Winterbourne Stoke
Down

A 410 **B** **C** 11 **D**

STRANG
STRANG

F A R G O

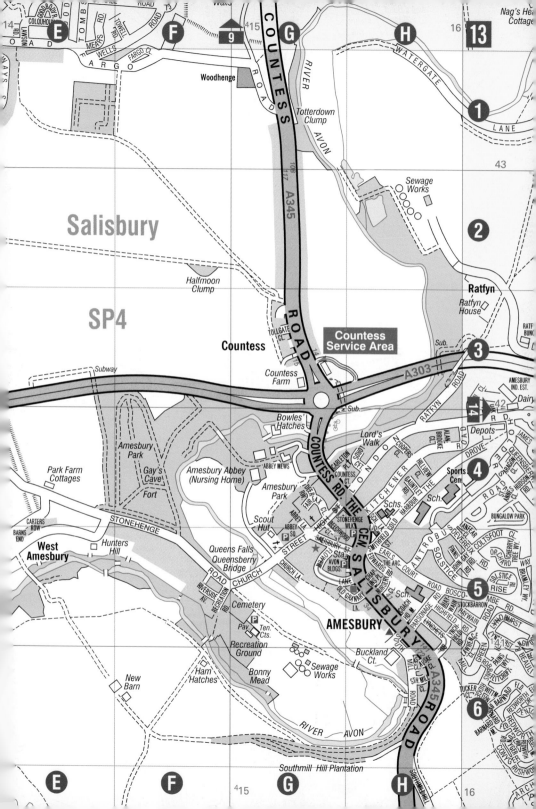

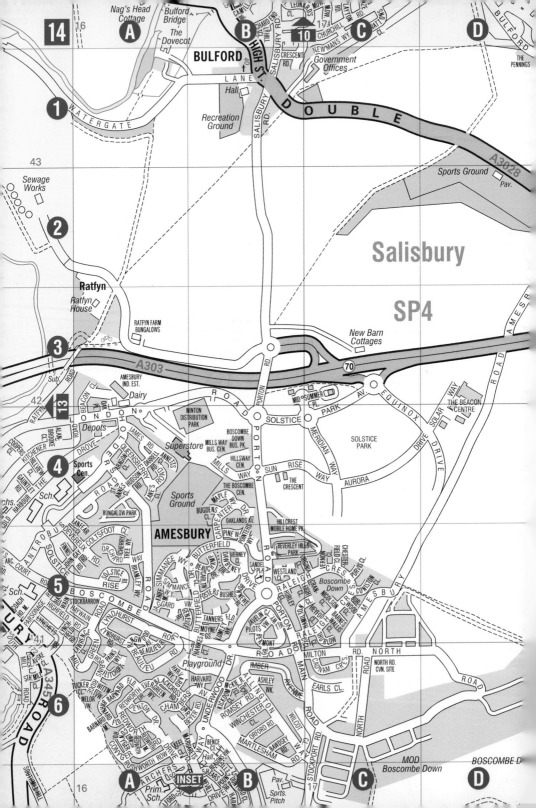

WING ST.
NEW HAIG RD.
E Wing Barracks
Kiwi Barracks
F
Kiwi Barracks
HUBERT HAMI...
Ground
19
SIGNAL RD.
RAWLINSON RD.
RAWLINSON RD.
BOND ROAD
MILNE
GUNNER ST.
MARLBOROUGH ROAD
WYVERN
ROAD
†
BULFORD CAMP
Ten. Cts.
Ten. Cts.
HEADQUARTERS
HEADQUARTERS RD.
Picton Barracks
G
MELBOURNE GS.
ADELAIDE CLO.
CAIRNS RD.
BROAD GS.
BRYS GS.
CANBERRA RD.
DARWIN DR.
ROAD
H
Stephen's Mound
4 20

11

Clay Mould
1

¹43

H E D G E S

2
Beacon Hill
Beacon Hanging

A303

3
Margaret's Wood

42

A L L I N G T O N

Beaconhill Gorse
Beacon Hill Farm

4

Reservoir (covered)

T R A C K

Boscombe Down West

ARCHERS WY.
SPEARS
DUNFORD CL.
DUNFORD DR.
HAM BROOK CT.
Prim. Sch.
INFILL
DRIVE
POINT
HARAGON DR.
HOLLOWAY
KILFORD CLOSE
CL.
HOLLOWAY
CL.
PENNY LA.
Pav.
Pav.
Sprts. Pitch
Sports Grd.
ROAD
5

Pav.

Salisbury SP4

¹40

STOCKPORT
STOCKPORT PARK

6

BOSCOMBE DOWN AIRFIELD

RFIELD
8
E
F
16
G
H
4 17

E F **TIDWORTH** **ROAD** 19 G H LADYWAY 420 37

Birdlymes Fm.
Birdlime Cottages
Birdlime Farm
Parkland
Rec. Grd.
Mount Pleasant

SOUTHBOURNE
MALVERN
SOUTHBOURNE CL.
N. HALSEN
BEECH CL.
THE BOURNE
HORE FIELD
Swanson
Tresillian

Prim. Sch.
PORTON
Ford
High View
Bonaker Farm

The Lines
Hall
Hall
BULLER PK.
Garden Centre

BIFORD GS.
DONNER
NICHOLSON
PARSONS CL.

1

West Gomeldon
The White House
Ford
Bourne

BOURNE VALLEY CL.
ROAD

ROAD

36

2

Downs Farm
SPIRE VIEW PARK
Sch.
GOMELDON
EAST

HIGH
GOMELDON
ROAD

3

East Gomeldon

rn Mill
emans ner
SMITH
LADYSMITH CL.
LADYS. WY.
HILLSIDE DR.
BROADFIELD RD.
BROADFIELD CL.
SMITH
HERMAN

GOMELDON
ROAD

St. Judes
Broadfield Farm

4

WINTERBOURNE GUNNER

GOMELDON
SALT LA.
HORSE BARROW
LLOYD
GRN.
HORNEY
DOWN

135

TRENCHARD AV.
RA GAR
ALLENBY RD.
laying Field
FIGSBURY RIDGE
Barracks

5

Thorny Down

6

ROAD 420 34

E F **23** 19 G H ROAD 420

Figsbury Ring Fort

34

A   **B**   09   **C**   **D**

Heath Hill

Mill Farm

South Newton Mill

Mill Farm Cottages

1

Custom Bottom

Sewage Works

RIVER WYLE

A36

Folly Farm

Heath Wood

Grovely Wood

2

FIRST BROAD DR.

Grovely Down

33

Grim's Ditch

Chilhampton

Chilhampton Farm

Grovely Hill

3

OX

DROVE

Seven Hatches

Plough Cottage

A36

Ugford Red Buildings

4

ELIZABETH RD

OLIVIER RD

PHILIP

WISHFORD ROAD

132

Reservoir (covered)

ROAD WATER

Grovely Riding Sch.

SP2

WARMINSTER RD. QUEEN'S K.

BARNACK IND. GEN.

KING BUS.

5

THE HOLLOWS

Ditchampton

DITCHAMPTON ROAD

WILTON

Milford Park School

Victoria FLATS

Playing Field

WILEY TER

RIVERSIDE

THE

Pav.

CASTLE KEEP

Com. Cen.

St. JOHN'S SQ

St. John's Priory

Pembroke Ct.

CHURCHILL

RUSSELL

SQ

NORTH STREET

KINGSBURY SQ

WYLYE LODGE

SHORT LANDS

78

VICTORIA

St. John's St.

FLORENCE MEAD CT.

FLORENCE CT.

SADDLERS

SHASTON

CROW LA.

WEST

ST.

22

6

A30

Ugford

SHAFTESBURY ROAD

85

Cemy.

ST. SILVER ST.

MINST

Lib.

P.

31

RIVER NADDER

A   **B**   09   **C**   **D**

08

26

Kennel

Bulbridge

Bull Bri.

Mill

Wilton House

R. NADDER

SOUTH

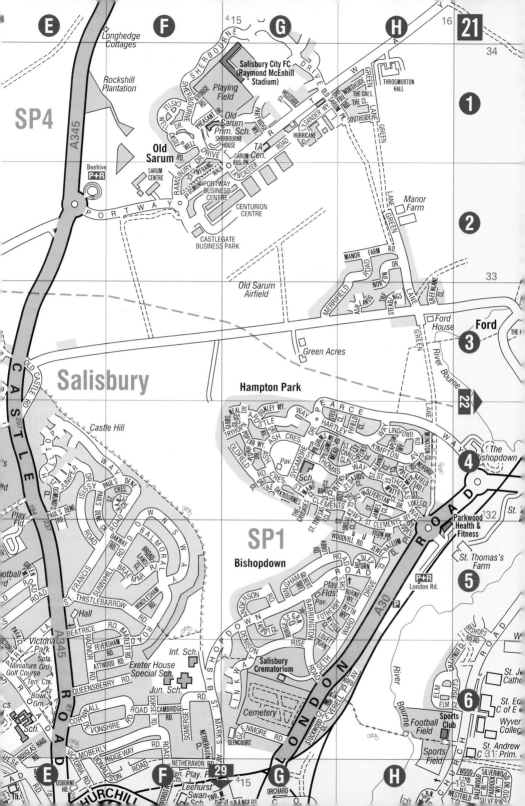

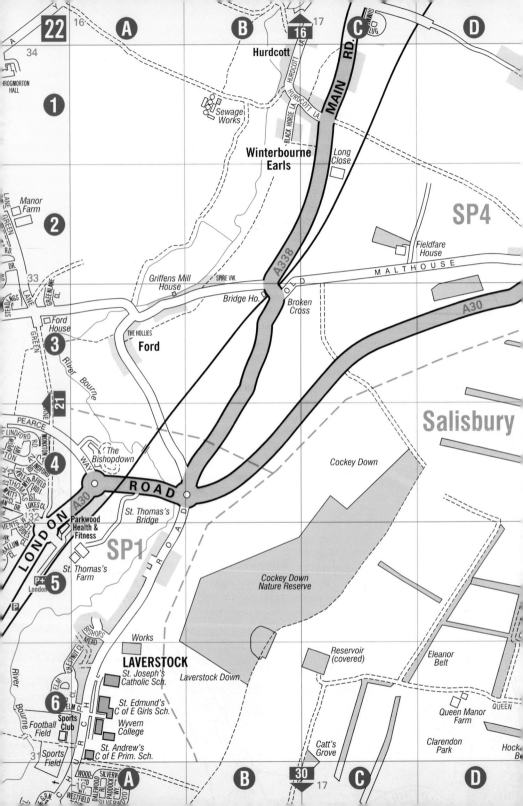

Figsbury Ring Fort

P

Paddock House Farm

ROAD

1

A30

Warren Down Farm

2

Hill View

33

LANE

Highfield House   Vimy Ridge   Stockbottom Farm

Spire View

Earlswood

3

24

4

132

King Edward's Belt

SP5

Savage's Belts

Fussells Lodge Farm

5

Goose Neck Belt

Carverel Copse

6   Four Cotts.

MANOR   ROAD

QUEEN MANOR ROAD

Savage's Farm

Fairoak Cotts. 31

Pumphouse Belt

Savage's Farm Cottages

Warner's Copse

Fairoak Copse

een or Belt

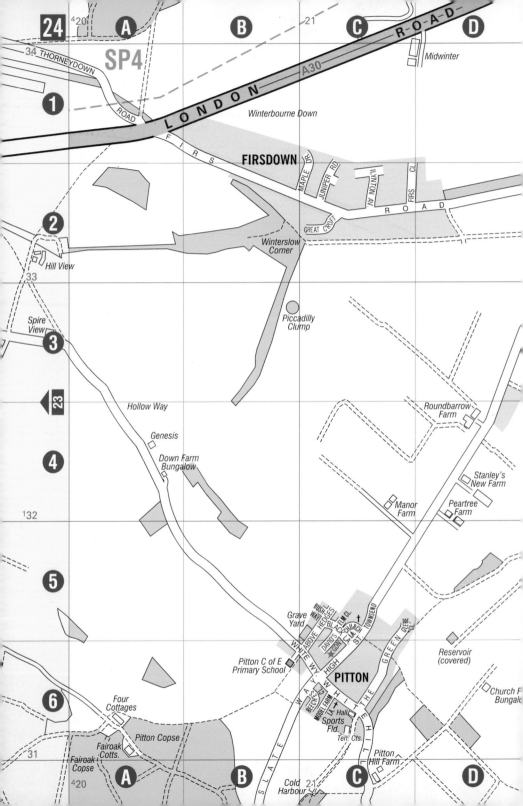

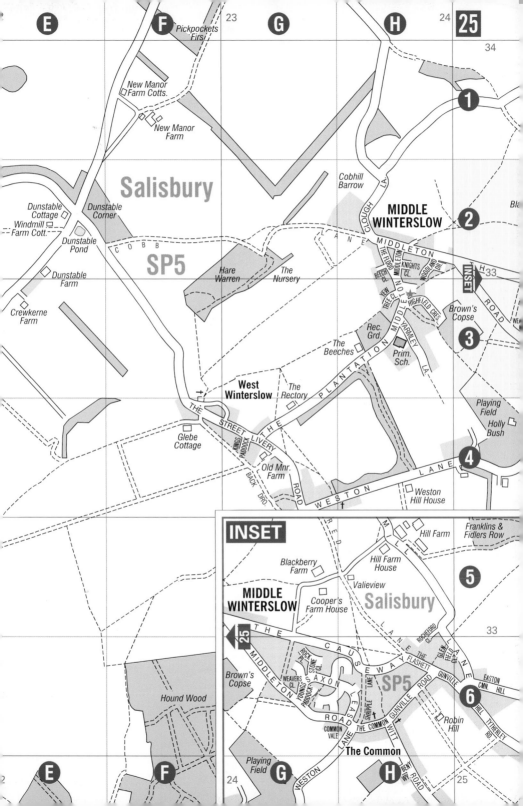

Pickpockets
Firs

New Manor
Farm Cotts.

New Manor
Farm

Salisbury

Cobhill
Barrow

Dunstable
Cottage

Dunstable
Corner

**MIDDLE
WINTERSLOW**

Windmill
Farm Cott.

Dunstable
Pond

SP5

Hare
Warren

The
Nursery

MIDDLETON

THE FLOOD

MIDDLETON

KNIGHTS
CL.

WOODLAND
DRI.

BEECH CL.

INSET

H 33

Dunstable
Farm

COBB

NEW
TREE CL.

HIGHFIELD CRES.

Brown's
Copse

WE

Crewkerne
Farm

MIDDLETON

Rec.
Grd.

YARMLEY

Prim.
Sch.

The
Beeches

ROAD

**West
Winterslow**

The
Rectory

PLANTATION

LA.

Playing
Field

Holly
Bush

Glebe
Cottage

THE STREET

LIVERY

YOUNG'S
PADDOCK

THE

Old Mnr.
Farm

ROAD

BACK DRO.

WESTON

LANE

Weston
Hill House

RED

INSET

Hill Farm

Franklins &
Fidlers Row

MILL

Blackberry
Farm

Hill Farm
House

Valieview

**MIDDLE
WINTERSLOW**

Cooper's
Farm House

Salisbury

25

THE CAUSEWAY

ROCHFORD

ROAD

GLENFIELD

THE
FLASHETT

GUNVILLE

EASTON
CMN.
HILL

MIDDLETON

THE

SAXON

WEAVERS
CL.

ROCK
STONE CL.

YOUNG'S
PADDOCK

SHRIPPLE
LANE

LEASE

GUNVILLE ROAD

SP5

Brown's
Copse

ROAD

TITHERLEY
RD.

Robin
Hill

Hound Wood

LANE

THE COMMON

WITT

COMMON
VALE

The Common

Playing
Field

WESTON

BENY
WAY
ROAD

33

34

35

36

25

ROAD

33

E   **F**   **G**   **H** **WILTON ROAD** A36

ROAD

NETHERHAMPTON A3094

River Wylye

WILTON PARK

Daye House

Quidhampton

ALBION BUNGALOWS

THE ALDERS

Boys Meadow Withybed

Purchase Plantation

BEMERTON FARM

SKEW ROAD

FOOT'S HILL

Sports Ground

Salisbury & South Wiltshire Sports Club

Cricket Ground

Prim. Sch.

Rec. Grd.

1

2

Netherhampton Farm

SOUTH BANK

Netherhampton

Netherhampton House

Belle Vue Cotts.

Netherhampton Business Centre

RACE PLAIN ROAD

The Strip

NETHERHAMPTON

A3094

ROAD

28

Meadow Dairy Cottages

3

4

Club House

Nursery

Grove's Folly

Down Barn

29

SALISBURY & SOUTH WILTS GOLF COURSE

erhampton Down

SALISBURY RACECOURSE

FOXMORE DROVE

5

6

Little Acre

SHAFTESBURY DROVE LANE

(SHASTON)

DROVE 28

E   **F**   33   **G**   **H**

11

Bake Farm Bungalows

Bake Farm Cottages

12

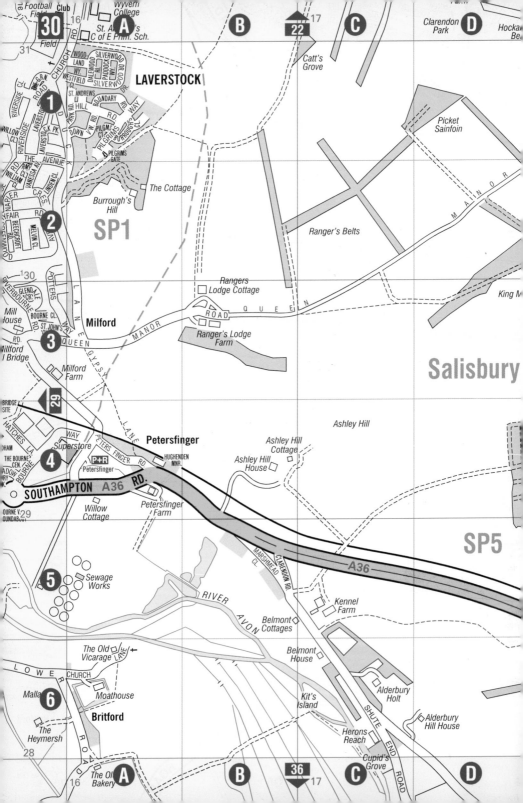

E 18
ore

Savage's
Farm

F

19

23

G

H

4'20

Pumphouse
Belt

Savage's Farm
Cottages

ROAD

Warner's
Copse

Fairoak
Copse

1

Home Copse

Great Netley
Copse

Beechy Dean
Copse

2

Clarendon Palace
(remains of)
ale

Great Gilbert's
Copse

Little Netley
Copse

'30

or Hill

Little Gilbert's
Copse

Crendle Bottom
Copse

3

Piper's
Cottages

Grimsditch
Copse

Grimsditch
Plantation

Clarendon
Park

Long Copse

4

Beech Tree
Cottage

29

Hendon
Copse

Canon
Copse

Furze Ground
Copse

Rag Withybed

Morley
lantation

Brickkiln
Copse

5

Clarendon Park

The Slip

The Rookery

Subway

Brick Kiln
Cottages

Great
Withybed

Clarendon
House

A36

Willow
Bed

Dairy
Cottages

Alderbury
Lodge

6

CLARENDON

28

8

E

F

37

nds

G

H

ROAD

Walden

Hole Farm

19

4'20

Bake Farm
Bungalows

Bake Farm
Cottages

Bake
Farm

1

2

A354

Salisbury

ombe
arm

Old Foundry
Cottages

Drove
House

Cawdon

27

SP5

Meadows

3

Homington
House

Homington Down

ombe.
Cotts.

STRATFORD TONY ROAD

DROVE CL.

LANE

SALISBURY RD.

MARSH LA.

Watercress
Beds

34

WILLOWMEAD CL.

**COOMBE
BISSETT**

Cranborne
Farm

OLD BLANDFORD RD.

THE
ROOKERY

THORNE
NEEDLE PL.

HOMINGTON

Ford

4

Ford

Ford

Ford

ROAD

R O A D

SHEP

SHUTTS LA.

SPOKES BRIDGE

MEADENS LA.

HOMINGTON

ROAD

LOWE 26

Coombe Bisset
C of E Prim. Sch.

Hall

DROVE

Burial
Ground

Huminga

5

SHUTTS LANE

PENNINGS LANE

A354

Highfield

6

BLANDFORD

Coombe Bissett Down

GYPSY LANE

THE BEECHES

Nature
Reserve

Lower
Coombe
Farm

125
Homington Dow

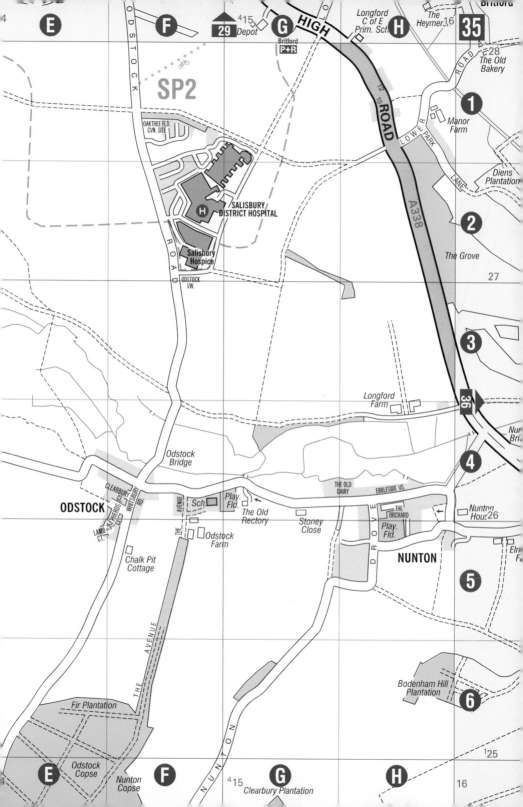

36

28

27

26

125

16

A   B   30   C   D
1   2   3   4   5   6

He
16 LOWER RD.

The Old Bakery

Manor Farm

LOWER PARK LANE

Diens Plantation

The Grove

27

A338

NUNTON

Nunton House

Elm Tree Farm

THE ORCHARD

VS.

Longford Park

Kennel Lodge

Lower Farm

Longford Mill

Nunton Bridge

35

Sports Field
Pav.

BODENHAM

Laurel Cottages

H NEW HALL PRIVATE HOSPITAL

Inveresk House

Bodenham Hill Plantation

Green Pastures

THE HIGHWAY

Charlton Plantation

Matrimony Farm House

Cupid's Grove

30

17

HUTE

RIVER AVON

Avon Turn

Brickkiln Plantation

Great Island

Longford Castle

Home Farm

Alderbury Meadows

Horse Hams

RIVER AVON

Great Hams

Pound Piece Withybed

Ford

17

Hill House

Shute End

SHUTE END

Shute End Copse

Lower Bigmans Copse

Alward House

Northfie Withybe

Sta Cott

ROAD WITHE

SILVER

Low Loo

Nythef Cops

Withe

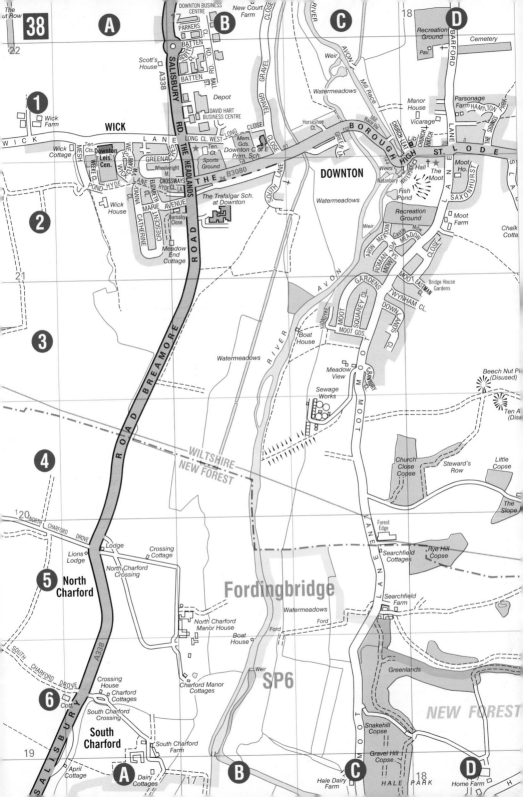

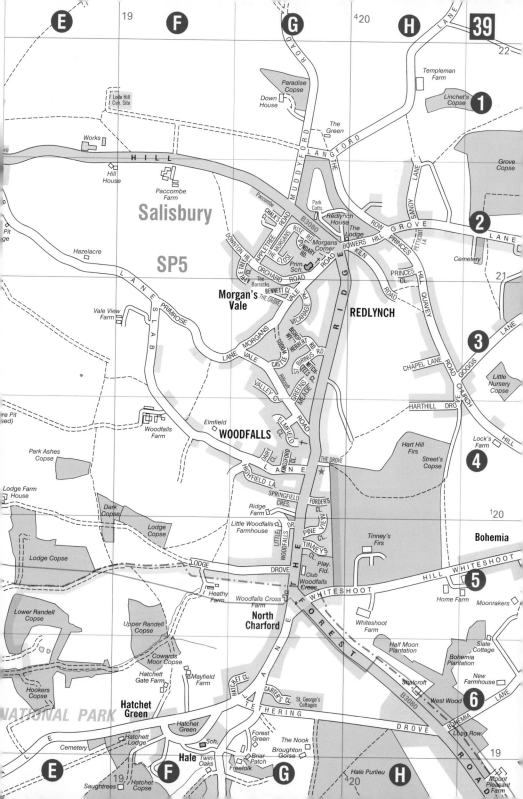

Grid references: **E** 19 **F** **G** 4 20 **H** LANE **39** 22

1
Templeman Farm
Linchet's Copse
Lode Hill Cvn. Site
Works
Paradise Copse
Down House
The Green
Grove Copse

2
HILL
Hill House
Paccombe Farm
Park Cotts.
Redlynch House
The Lodge
Morgans Corner
BOWERS
Cemetery
21

Salisbury
SP5
Hazelacre
CHALK'S CL.
APPLETREE
MORGANS
THE CLOSE
RISE
Paccombe
DOWNTON HILL
THREE CUP CL.
ORCHARD
The Barracks
BENNETT CL.
THE DROVE
Prim. Sch.
BOUNDARY RD.
MORGANS RD.
VALE
Park Cotts.
KILN
GROVE
PRINCES HILL
PETTICOR LA.
SANDY ROW
THE
LANGFORD ROAD
MUDDYFORD ROAD
B3080

Morgan's Vale
REDLYNCH
PRINCES CL.
PRINCES HILL
QUAVEY ROAD
RIDGE
VICARAGE PK.
BISHOP'S WY.
HEBER RD.
CASTLE HIGHRD.
SODOM LANE
ST BIRINUS RD.
GREENS MEADE
MITCH. CL.
ST GILES CL.
MORGANS VALE LANE
PRIMROSE LANE
SLAB LANE
Vale View Farm

3
CHAPEL LANE
GOGGS LANE
Little Nursery Copse
HARTHILL DRO.
CHURCH HILL
VALLEY CL.
HIGHRD.

WOODFALLS
Elmfield
ELMFIELD CL.
DAIRY CL.
KINGSFORD CL.
ROAD
HIGHFIELD LA.
Woodfalls Farm
THE DROVE
Hart Hill Firs
Street's Copse
Lock's Farm
CHURCH HILL

4
Park Ashes Copse
Lodge Farm House
Dark Copse
Lodge Copse
Lodge Copse
SPRINGFIELD CRES.
Ridge Farm
Little Woodfalls Farmhouse
LITTLE WOODFALLS DR.
FORDER'S CL.
PINE VIEW CL.
Tinney's CL.
Tinney's Firs
Play. Fld.
1 20
Bohemia

5
Lower Randell Copse
Upper Randell Copse
THE LODGE DROVE
Heathy Farm
Woodfalls Cross Farm
Woodfalls Cross
Club
THE
ANNE
FOREST
WHITESHOOT
WHITESHOOT
Whiteshoot Farm
HILL
Home Farm
Moonrakers
Half Moon Plantation

North Charford
Cowards Moor Copse
Hatchett Gate Farm
Mayfield Farm
HATCHET CL.
Whiteshoot Farm
Slate Cottage
Bohemia Plantation
New Farmhouse
Shalcroft
West Wood
B3080

6
Hookers Copse
Hatchet Green
Hatchett Lodge
Cemetery
Hatchet Green
CARTER'S CL.
TETHERING DROVE
St. George's Cottages
Sch.
Forest Green
The Nook
Broughton Gorse
Hale Purlieu
BOHEMIA LANE ROAD
Long Row
19
Mount Pleasant Farm

Hale
Twin Oaks
Briar Patch
Freefolk
Saughtrees
Hatchet Copse

NATIONAL PARK
E 19 **F** **G** 4 20 **H**

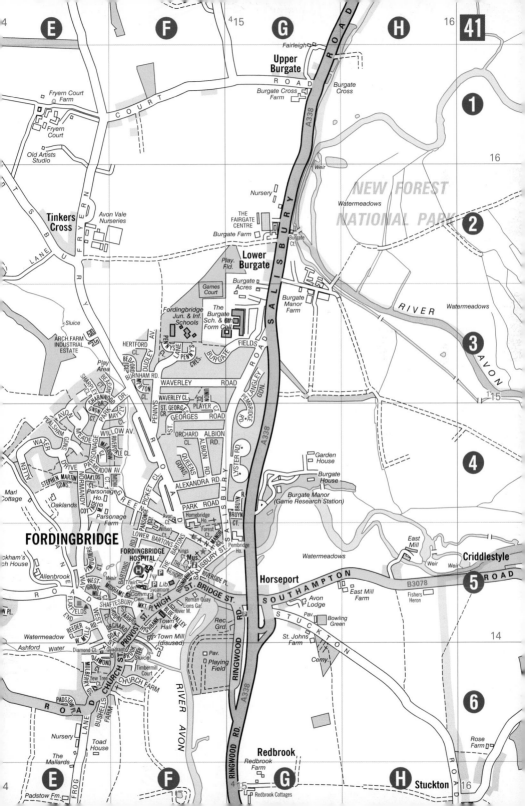

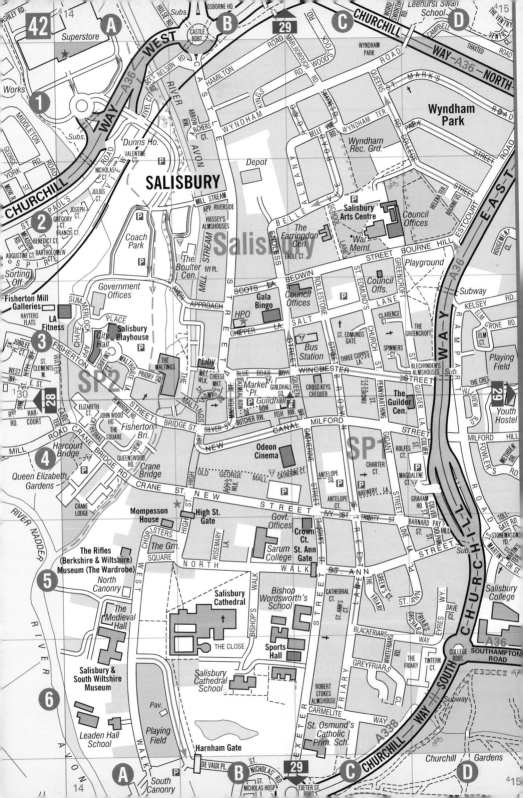

INDEX

Including Streets, Places & Areas, Hospitals etc., Industrial Estates,
Selected Flats & Walkways, Service Areas, Stations and Selected Places of Interest.

HOW TO USE THIS INDEX

1. Each street name is followed by its Postcode District, then by its Locality abbreviation(s) and then by its map reference;
e.g. **Alanbrooke Rd.** SP4: Lark . . . .6B **8** is in the SP4 Postcode District and the Larkhill Locality and is to be found in square 6B on page **8**.
The page number is shown in bold type.

2. A strict alphabetical order is followed in which Av., Rd., St., etc. (though abbreviated) are read in full and as part of the street name;
e.g. **Avon Dr.** appears after **Avondown Rd.** but before **Avondyke**

3. Streets and a selection of flats and walkways that cannot be shown on the mapping, appear in the index with the thoroughfare to which they are
connected shown in brackets; e.g. **Alexander Ho.** SP9: Tid . . . .3F **3** (off Sidbury Circular Rd.)

4. Addresses that are in more than one part are referred to as not continuous.

5. Places and areas are shown in the index in **BLUE TYPE** and the map reference is to the actual map square in which the town centre or area is located
and not to the place name shown on the map; e.g. **BULFORD** 6B **10**

6. An example of a selected place of interest is **Fordingbridge Mus.** 5F **41**

7. An example of a station is **Salisbury Station (Rail)** . . . .2D **28**, also included is **Park & Ride**.
e.g. **Beehive (Park & Ride)** 2E **21**

8. Service Areas are shown in the index in **BOLD CAPITAL TYPE**; e.g. **COUNTESS SERVICE AREA** 3G **13**

9. An example of a Hospital, Hospice or selected Healthcare facility is **FORDINGBRIDGE HOSPITAL** 5F **41**

10. Map references for entries that appear on large scale page **42** are shown first, with small scale map references shown in brackets;
e.g. **Bedwin St.** SP1: Sal 2C **42** (2F **29**)

GENERAL ABBREVIATIONS

App. : Approach	**Gdn.** : Garden	**Ri.** : Rise
Av. : Avenue	**Gdns.** : Gardens	**Rd.** : Road
Bri. : Bridge	**Ga.** : Gate	**Rdbt.** : Roundabout
Bldgs. : Buildings	**Grn.** : Green	**Shop.** : Shopping
Bungs. : Bungalows	**Gro.** : Grove	**Sth.** : South
Bus. : Business	**Ho.** : House	**Sq.** : Square
Cen. : Centre	**Ind.** : Industrial	**St.** : Street
Cl. : Close	**Info.** : Information	**Ter.** : Terrace
Comn. : Common	**La.** : Lane	**Trad.** : Trading
Cotts. : Cottages	**Lit.** : Little	**Va.** : Vale
Ct. : Court	**Mnr.** : Manor	**Vw.** : View
Cres. : Crescent	**Mkt.** : Market	**Vs.** : Villas
Cft. : Croft	**Mdw.** : Meadow	**Vis.** : Visitors
Dr. : Drive	**M.** : Mews	**Wlk.** : Walk
E. : East	**Mus.** : Museum	**W.** : West
Est. : Estate	**Nth.** : North	**Yd.** : Yard
Fld. : Field	**Pk.** : Park	
Flds. : Fields	**Pl.** : Place	

LOCALITY ABBREVIATIONS

Alderb : **Alderbury**	Fordi : **Fordingbridge**	Per D : **Perham Down**
Alderh : **Alderholt**	God : **Godshill**	Pet : **Petersfinger**
All : **Allington**	Gom : **Gomeldon**	Pit : **Pitton**
Ame : **Amesbury**	Gt S : **Great Shoddesden**	Por : **Porton**
Bar St M : **Barford St Martin**	Hale : **Hale**	Quid : **Quidhampton**
Bid : **Biddesden**	Hax : **Haxton**	Rede : **Redenham**
Bis : **Bishopstone**	Hom : **Homington**	Red : **Redlynch**
Bre : **Breamore**	Hur : **Hurdcott**	Roc : **Rockbourne**
Brig : **Brigmerston**	Idm : **Idmiston**	Sal : **Salisbury**
Brit : **Britford**	Kim : **Kimpton**	San : **Sandleheath**
Bul : **Bulford**	Lark : **Larkhill**	Strat C : **Stratford sub Castle**
Bul C : **Bulford Camp**	Lav : **Laverstock**	Stru : **Stuckton**
Bur : **Burgate**	Lit S : **Little Shoddesden**	Tid : **Tidworth**
Charl S : **Charlton-All-Saints**	Lwr W : **Lower Woodford**	W Ame : **West Amesbury**
Coombe B : **Coombe Bissett**	Lud : **Ludgershall**	W Gri : **West Grimstead**
Dow : **Downton**	Midd W : **Middle Winterslow**	W Win : **West Winterslow**
Dur : **Durrington**	Mil : **Milston**	Whad : **Whaddon**
E Win : **East Winterslow**	Mor V : **Morgan's Vale**	Wilt : **Wilton**
Enf : **Enford**	N'avon : **Netheravon**	Wint D : **Winterbourne Dauntsey**
Fab : **Faberstown**	N'ton : **Netherhampton**	Wint E : **Winterbourne Earls**
Fig : **Figheldean**	Nun : **Nunton**	Wint G : **Winterbourne Gunner**
Firs : **Firsdown**	Ods : **Odstock**	Woodf : **Woodfalls**
Ford : **Ford**	Old S : **Old Sarum**	Woodg : **Woodgreen**

A

	Abbotts Cl. SP9: Tid .4F 3	Alanbrooke Cl. SP4: Ame 4H 13
	Abbotts Rd. SP9: Tid .4F 3	Alanbrooke Rd. SP4: Lark 6B 8
	ABLINGTON 5H 7	Albany Rd. SP1: Sal 2C 42 (2F 29)
Abbatt Cl. SP11: Lud .1G 5	Above Hedges SP5: Pit 6C 24	Albany Ter. SP2: Wilt 6D 18
Abbess Cl. SP4: Ame 6H 13	Adampur Rd. SP9: Tid 6D 2	Albion Bungs. SP2: Quid 6G 19
Abbey La. SP4: Ame 4G 13	Adam's Cl. SP11: Per D 5C 4	Albion Rd. SP6: Fordi 4F 41
Abbey M. SP4: Ame 4G 13	Addison Sq. SP4: Dur 5H 9	**ALDERBURY** 2E 37
Abbey Sq. SP4: Ame 4G 13	Adelaide Cl. SP4: Bul C 1G 15	Alderholt Mill 5A 40
Abbot Rd. SP1: Sal .5G 21	Agra Rd. SP9: Tid 6D 2	Alderholt Rd. SP6: San 5A 40

Alders, The SP2: Quid 6G 19
Aldworth Dr. SP1: Sal 4G 21
Alexander Ho. SP9: Tid 3F 3
  (off Sidbury Circular Rd.)
Alexandra Cl. SP2: Sal 6A 20
Alexandra Dr. SP2: Sal 6B 20
Alexandra Rd. SP6: Fordi 4F 41
Allenby Rd. SP4: Wint G 5E 17
Allen Water Dr. SP6: Fordi 4E 41
Allington Track SP4: All, Ame 3E 15
Allington Way SP4: Ame 6B 14
ALTON 6G 7
AMESBURY 5G 13
Amesbury Ho. SP9: Tid 5G 13
  (off Kennet Rd.)
Amesbury Ind. Est. SP4: Ame 3A 14
Amesbury Rd. SP4: Ame, Bul, Cul 5C 14
Amesbury Sports & Community Cen. 4A 14
Ancient Way SP2: Sal 5F 29
Anderson Rd. SP1: Sal 5G 21
Andover La. SP11: Gt S 4H 5
Andover Rd. SP11: Fab, Lud, Rede 1D 4
Andrew Cl. SP4: Dur 5H 9
Andrews Way SP2: Sal 6D 28
Angler Rd. SP2: Sal 4A 20
Anne Cres. SP4: Dur 5H 9
Annetts Cl. SP4: Ame 4A 14
Antelope Cl. SP1: Sal 4C 42 (3F 29)
Antelope Sq. SP1: Sal 4C 42
Antrim Cl. SP4: Bul C 5E 11
Antrobus Rd. SP4: Ame 5H 13
Apostle Way SP1: Sal 4G 21
Appleshaw Way SP1: Sal 4H 21
  SP11: Per D 5C 4
Appletree Cl. SP5: Mor V 2G 39
Appletree Rd. SP5: Mor V 2G 39
Aragon Cl. SP4: Ame 4A 14
Arcade, The SP4: Ame 5H 13
Archers Ct. SP1: Sal 1B 42 (1E 29)
Archers Way SP4: Ame 5G 15
Arch Farm Ind. Est. SP6: Fordi 3E 41
Armitage Sq. SP4: Lark 6B 8
Armstrong Ho. SP2: Sal 5B 28
Arnott Cl. SP9: Tid 5G 3
Ashburn Pl. SP6: Fordi 5E 41
Ash Cl. SP9: Tid 4H 3
Ash Cres. SP1: Sal 4G 21
Ashdown Ter. SP9: Tid 6G 3
Ashfield Rd. SP2: Sal 2C 28
Ashfield Trad. Est. SP2: Sal 2C 28
ASHFORD 5D 40
Ashford Cl. SP6: Fordi 5D 40
Ashford Rd. SP6: Fordi 6C 40
Ashford Works Ind. Est. SP6: Fordi 5D 40
Ashlands SP4: Ford 3H 21
Ashley Ct. SP2: Sal 1D 28
Ashley Rd. SP2: Sal 1A 42 (1D 28)
Ashley Wlk. SP4: Ame 6B 14
Assheton Cl. SP9: Tid 4G 3
Assisi Rd. SP1: Sal 4E 21
Aston Mead SP1: Sal 6G 21
Astor Cres. SP11: Lud 1D 4
Attwood Rd. SP1: Sal 6E 21
Auchinleck Ho. SP9: Tid 3F 3
  (off Sidbury Circular Rd.)
Auckland Rd. SP4: Bul C 5G 11
Augustine Ct. SP2: Sal 2A 42
Aurora Dr. SP4: Ame 4C 14
Australian Av. SP2: Sal 1B 28
Avenue, The 2B 12
Avenue, The SP1: Lav 1H 29
  SP1: Sal 2G 29
  SP2: Wilt 6E 19
  SP4: Dur 5H 9
  SP4: Lwr W 1G 19
  SP4: Por 1F 17
  SP5: Ods 6F 35
  (not continuous)
  SP9: Tid 6F 3
Avon App. SP1: Sal 3B 42 (2E 29)
Avon Bank SP4: Fig 6H 7
Avon Cl. SP6: Fordi 4F 41
Avondown Rd. SP4: Dur 5A 10
Avon Dr. SP5: Alderb 3G 37
Avondyke SP5: Dow 3C 38
Avon Mead Ct. SP4: Dur 5A 10
Avon Meade SP6: Fordi 4E 41
Avon Mdw. SP5: Dow 2C 38
Avon Pk. SP4: N'avon 2F 7
Avon Pl. SP1: Sal 3G 29

Avon Rd. SP4: Bul C 6G 11
  SP9: Tid 6F 3
Avonstoke Cl. SP4: Ame 6H 13
Avon Ter. SP2: Sal 1D 28
Avon Valley Local Nature Reserve 6D 20
Ayleswade Rd. SP2: Sal 5E 29
Ayrshire Cl. SP2: Sal 4A 20

B

Back Drove SP5: Midd W 4G 15
Baghdad Rd. SP4: Bul C 5G 11
Ballymena Way SP4: Bul C 5E 11
Balmoral Rd. SP1: Sal 5F 21
Bank, The SP4: Wint D 5D 16
Barber's La. SP5: Hom 4A 22
Barford La. SP5: Dow 1D 38
Barnaby Cl. SP5: Dow 2B 38
Barnack Bus. Cen. SP1: Sal 3G 29
Barnack Ind. Cen. SP2: Wilt 4D 18
Barnard Fld. SP4: Ame 6A 14
Barnard M. SP4: Ame 6A 14
Barnards Hill Dr. SP2: Sal 5A 20
Barnard St. SP1: Sal 5D 42 (3F 29)
Barnes Wallis Cl. SP4: Ame 5C 14
Barns End SP4: W Ame 5E 13
Baroda Rd. SP9: Tid 6D 2
Barracks, The SP5: Mor V 3G 39
Barrington Rd. SP1: Sal 5G 21
Bartholomew Ct. SP2: Sal 2A 42
Bartlett Rd. SP1: Sal 5F 21
Bartons, The SP6: Fordi 5F 41
Bartons Rd. SP6: Fordi 5F 41
Batten Rd. SP5: Dow 1B 38
Bawdsey Rd. SP4: Ame 6B 14
Bayeux M. SP9: Tid 4F 3
Bays Cl. SP2: Sal 2D 28
Bazaar Rd. SP9: Tid 6D 2
Beacon Centre, The SP4: Ame 3D 14
Beacon Cl. SP4: Ame 3A 14
Beacon Ct. SP6: Fordi 3E 41
Beacon Hill Rd. SP4: Bul C 5H 11
Beamont Way SP4: Ame 5B 14
Beard Ct. SP11: Lud 1F 5
Beatrice Rd. SP1: Sal 5E 21
Beauchamp Dr. SP4: Ame 5B 14
Beaulieu Rd. SP4: Ame 6A 14
Becket Way SP1: Sal 2H 29
Bedford Cl. SP4: Por 1F 17
Bedford Rd. SP2: Sal 1C 28
Bedwin St. SP1: Sal 2C 42 (2F 29)
Beech Cl. SP4: Por 1F 17
  SP5: Midd W 2H 25
Beechcroft Rd. SP1: Lav 2H 29
Beeches, The SP1: Sal 3G 29
  SP5: Coombe B 6F 33
Beeches Cl. SP5: Pit 6C 24
Beech Hill Rd. SP9: Tid 4H 3
Beechwood SP6: Fordi 5D 40
Beechwood Ct. SP4: Ame 4G 13
Beehive (Park & Ride) 2E 21
Belgrave Cres. SP9: Tid 5H 3
Bellamy La. SP1: Sal 3G 29
Belle Vue Cotts. SP2: N'ton 3G 27
Belle Vue Rd. SP1: Sal 2B 42 (2F 29)
Bell La. SP2: Wilt 6D 18
Bell Rd. SP4: Lark 4C 8
Bell St. SP11: Lud 1F 5
Bemerton Farm SP2: Sal 1H 27
BEMERTON HEATH 6A 20
Bemerton Heath &
  Barnard's Folly Local Nature Reserve
  ....5A 20
Bence Ct. SP4: Ame 6B 14
Benedict Ct. SP2: Sal 2A 42
Bengal Rd. SP4: Bul C 6F 11
Benin Rd. SP11: Per D 5C 4
Bennett Cl. SP5: Mor V 3G 39
Bentley Way SP5: Midd W 6H 25
Berkshire Rd. SP2: Sal 4C 28
Berry Cl. SP4: N'avon 2F 7
Berrysfield Ct. SP11: Lud 1D 4
Beverley Hills Pk. SP4: Ame 5B 14
Beyer Rd. SP4: Ame 6B 14
Biddesden La. SP11: Bid, Lud 1G 5
Biddulph Rd. SP4: Lark 5E 9
Bingham Rd. SP1: Sal 5G 21
  SP4: Lark 5A 8
Birch Ct. SP9: Tid 4H 3
Birch Gro. SP5: Alderb 3G 37

Birchwood Dr. SP4: Dur 5A 10
BISHOPDOWN 5G 21
Bishopdown Rd. SP1: Sal 6F 21
Bishops Cl. SP9: Tid 6G 3
Bishops Ct. SP1: Sal 5G 21
  (off Bishopdown Rd.)
Bishops Dr. SP2: Sal 5D 28
Bishops Mead SP1: Lav 5A 22
Bishop's Wlk. SP1: Sal 5B 42 (3E 29)
Bishops Wordsworth Sports Hall & Fitness Suite
  ....6B 42 (4E 29)
Blackcross Rd. SP4: Ame 6A 14
Blackfriars Way SP1: Sal 5C 42 (3F 29)
Black Horse La. SP4: Wint E 1B 22
Black La. SP5: Pit 5C 24
Blackwell M. SP2: Sal 1D 28
Blakey Rd. SP1: Sal 3G 29
Blandford Rd. SP5: Coombe B 6F 33
Blechynden's Almshouses SP1: Sal 3D 42
Block Rd. SP4: Lark 5B 8
Blue Boar Row SP1: Sal 3B 42 (2E 29)
Blue Valley M. SP6: Fordi 5F 41
Blyth Way SP1: Sal 5H 21
Boathouse Meadow Bus. Pk. SP2: Sal 2B 28
BODENHAM 4B 36
Bodyworks Fitness Studio 5G 13
  (off Abbey Sq.)
BOHEMIA 5H 39
Bohemia La. SP5: Red 6H 39
  SP6: Hale 6H 39
Bonaker Cl. SP4: Por 1F 17
Bond St. SP4: Bul C 1E 15
Bonnewe Ri. SP4: Ame 5B 14
Borough, The SP5: Dow 2B 38
Boscombe Centre, The SP4: Ame 4B 14
Boscombe Down Bus. Pk. SP4: Ame 4B 14
Boscombe Rd. SP4: Ame 5H 13
Bouchers Way SP2: Sal 6E 29
Boundary Rd. SP1: Lav 1A 30
Bourne Av. SP1: Sal 1G 29
Bourne Centre, The SP1: Sal 4H 29
Bourne Cl. SP1: Sal 3H 29
Bourne Gdns. SP4: Por 1F 17
Bourne Hill SP1: Sal 2D 42 (2F 29)
Bourne Rd. SP9: Tid 5G 3
Bourne Valley Cl. SP4: Por 2G 17
Bourne Vs. SP1: Sal 2D 42
Bourne Way SP1: Sal 4H 29
Bourne Way Rdbt. SP5: Sal 4H 29
Bouverie Av. SP2: Sal 5D 28
Bouverie Av. Sth. SP2: Sal 6D 28
Bouverie Cl. SP2: Sal 5D 28
Bowdich Cl. SP4: Dur 5A 10
Bower Gdns. SP1: Sal 3G 29
Bower Hill Rd. SP1: Sal 1G 29
Bowerwood Cotts. SP6: Fordi 6C 40
Bowerwood Rd. SP6: Fordi 6C 40
Bowes Lyon Ct. SP2: Sal 6B 20
Brackenbury Rd. SP4: Lark 5A 8
Brambles, The SP1: Sal 1G 29
Bramley Way SP4: Ame 5A 14
Breamore Rd. SP5: Dow 5A 38
Brewery La. SP1: Sal 4C 42 (3F 29)
Brick Kiln La. SP5: Alderb 1E 37
Brick La. SP2: Sal 1A 28
Bridge Ho. Gdns. SP5: Dow 3D 38
Bridge St. SP1: Sal 4A 42 (3E 29)
  SP6: Fordi 5F 41
Bridgwater Cl. SP2: Sal 5B 28
Brier Ct. SP2: Sal 5A 20
BRIGMERSTON 2A 10
Brind Rd. SP4: Lark 4D 8
Brisbane Gdns. SP4: Bul C 1G 15
BRITFORD 6A 30
Britford (Park & Ride) 6G 29
Britford La. SP2: Sal 5F 29
Britford La. W. SP2: Sal 5E 29
Broadfield Cl. SP4: Gom 4F 17
Broadfield Rd. SP4: Gom 4F 17
Broadlands Cl. SP1: Sal 5F 21
Brook Ter. SP6: Fordi 6C 40
Brown St. SP1: Sal 3C 42 (3F 29)
Brunel Rd. SP2: Sal 3B 28
Bruyn Ct. SP6: Fordi 4G 41
Bruyn Rd. SP6: Fordi 4G 41
Brydges Rd. SP11: Lud 1E 5
Brympton Cl. SP6: Fordi 4D 40

Bugdens Cl. SP4: Ame 4B 14
BULBRIDGE 2B 26
Bulbridge Rd. SP2: Wilt 2B 26
BULFORD 6B 10
BULFORD CAMP 6F 11
Bulford Droveway SP4: Bul 6C 10
Bulford Hill SP4: Dur 6A 10
Bulford Kiwi 6H 11
Bulford Rd. SP4: Bul, Bul C 5C 10
  SP4: Dur 4H 9
  SP9: Tid 6E 3
Buller Pk. SP4: Por 2G 17
Bulls Drove SP11: Bid 1H 5
Bungalow Pk. SP4: Ame 4A 14
Burcombe La. SP2: Wilt 1B 26
Burford Av. SP2: Sal 5F 29
Burford La. SP2: Sal 5F 29
Burford Rd. SP2: Sal 5F 29
Burgate SP6: Bur 2G 41
Burgate Flds. SP6: Fordi 3F 41
Burgess Grn. SP1: Sal 5G 21
Burlington Wlk. SP9: Tid 5G 3
Burnet Way SP1: Sal 5H 21
Burnham Rd. SP6: Fordi 3F 41
Burroughs Cl. SP1: Lav 1A 30
Burwood Cl. SP4: Ame 5C 14
Bushells Farm SP6: Fordi 6E 41
Butcher Row SP1: Sal 4B 42
Butler Cl. SP2: Sal 5F 29
Butt Cl. SP11: Lud 1D 4
Butterfield Dr. SP4: Ame 5B 14
Butts Rd. SP1: Sal 1E 29
Butts Ter. SP2: Sal 1E 29
Butt St. SP11: Lud 1E 29
Byford Gdns. SP4: Por 1F 17
Byron Cl. SP11: Lud 1E 5
Byways Cl. SP1: Sal 3G 29

C

Cabul Rd. SP9: Tid 6E 3
Cadnam Cres. SP4: Ame 6C 14
Cambridge Rd. SP1: Sal 6F 21
Camilla Cl. SP4: Bul 6B 10
Camomile Dr. SP11: Lud 1E 5
Campbell Rd. SP1: Sal 1D 42 (1F 29)
Canadian Av. SP2: Sal 1B 28
Canal La. SP5: Alderb 3G 37
Canalside SP5: Alderb 3G 37
Canberra Dr. SP4: Bul C 6G 11
Canbury Cl. SP4: Ame 5B 14
Canons Cl. SP9: Tid 6G 3
Capulet Rd. SP1: Sal 5D 20
Carleton Cl. SP4: Ame 5B 14
Carleton Pl. SP4: Ame 4G 13
Carmelite Way SP1: Sal 6C 42 (4F 29)
Carnival Ho. SP2: Sal 6A 20
  (off Old Dairy Cl.)
Carpenter Dr. SP4: Ame 5B 14
Carrion Pond Drove SP2: Sal 5B 28
Carter's Cl. SP6: Hale 6G 39
Carters Row S: W Ame 4E 13
Castle Ct. SP11: Lud 1D 4
Castledown Bus. Pk. SP11: Lud 1C 4
Castledown Rd. SP11: Lud 2C 4
Castlegate Bus. Cen. SP4: Old S 2F 21
Castle Keep SP1: Strat C 5C 20
  SP2: Wilt 6D 18
Castle La. SP2: Wilt 6D 18
  SP5: Whad 3G 37
Castle Mdw. SP5: Dow 2C 38
Castle M. SP11: Lud 1D 4
  (off Crown La.)
Castle Rd. SP1: Sal 3E 21
Castle Rdbt. SP1: Sal 1B 42 (1E 29)
Castle St. SP1: Sal 1B 42 (1E 29)
  SP11: Sal 1D 4
Castle Well Dr. SP4: Old S 1F 21
Castle Well M. SP4: Old S 1F 21
  (off Castle Well Rd.)
Castle Well Rd. SP4: Old S 1F 21
Castle Woods SP5: Woodf 3G 39
Cathedral Ct. SP1: Sal 5C 42
Cathedral Views SP2: Sal 4A 42 (3E 29)
Catherine Ct. SP1: Sal 4B 42 (3E 29)
Catherine Cres. SP5: Dow 2A 38
Catherine St. SP1: Sal 4C 42 (3E 29)
Cator Rd. SP4: Lark 5B 8
Causeway, The SP5: Midd W 5G 25
Cecil Av. SP2: Sal 6E 29

Cecil Ter. SP2: Sal 2B 28
Cedar Cl. SP2: Sal 5H 19
Central St. SP11: Lud 1E 5
Centre, The SP4: Ame 4H 13
Centurion Cen. SP4: Old S 2G 21
Centurion Cl. SP2: Sal 1B 28
Chalk Down SP9: Tid 4H 3
Chalk's Cl. SP5: Mor V 4H 3
Challis Ct. SP11: Lud 1F 5
Chambers Av. SP4: Ame 6A 14
Chancery Cl. SP4: Ame 1C 28
Chandler Ct. SP9: Tid 4F 3
Chantry Cl. SP4: Dur 4H 9
Chantry Rd. SP2: Wilt .....
Chapel La. SP5: Red 2C 26
  SP11: Lud 3H 39
Chapel Pl. SP2: Sal 3A 42 (2E 29)
Chaplins Pl. SP4: Ame 5H 13
Charles Rd. SP4: Dur 5H 9
Charles St. SP2: Sal 2D 28
Charles Vesey Rd. SP9: Tid 4F 3
Charnwood Dr. SP6: Fordi 3E 41
Charnwood Rd. SP2: Sal 2C 28
Charter Ct. SP1: Sal 4C 42 (3F 29)
Chatham Cl. SP1: Sal 5D 20
Cheese Mkt. SP1: Sal 3B 42
Cherry Cl. SP2: Sal 2B 28
Cherry Orchard La. SP2: Sal 2B 28
Cherry Tree Av. SP9: Tid 4H 3
Cherry Tree Way SP4: Ame 5A 14
Cheshire Cl. SP2: Sal 5A 20
Chesterfield Cl. SP4: Ame 5C 14
Chestnut Av. SP4: N'avon 4F 7
  SP9: Tid 4G 3
Chestnut Cl. SP1: Lav 6H 21
Chestnut Cl. SP4: Dur 4A 10
Chestnut Ri. SP4: Hax 1F 7
Cheverell Av. SP1: Sal 6G 21
Chichester Cl. SP2: Sal 5F 29
CHILHAMPTON 2C 18
Chipper La. SP1: Sal 3B 42 (2E 29)
Chiselbury Gro. SP2: Sal 5E 29
Choristers Sq. SP1: Sal 5A 42 (3E 29)
CHOULSTON 3G 7
Choulston Cl. SP4: N'avon 2G 7
Christie Miller Rd. SP2: Sal 1C 28
Christopher Cl. SP2: Sal 6D 28
Church Farm SP6: Fordi 6F 41
CHURCHFIELDS 3C 28
Churchfields Rd. SP2: Sal 2C 28
Church Ga. SP11: Lud 1D 4
  (off Chapel La.)
Church Hatch SP5: Dow 1D 38
Church Hill SP5: Red 3H 39
Churchill Av. SP4: Bul 6B 10
Churchill Cl. SP9: Tid 3E 3
Churchill Ct. SP2: Wilt 6D 18
Churchill Way E. SP1: Sal 5D 42 (3F 29)
Churchill Way Nth. SP1: Sal 1C 42 (1E 29)
Churchill Way Sth. SP1: Sal 6C 42 (4F 29)
Churchill Way W. SP1: Sal 2A 42 (2D 29)
  SP2: Sal 2A 42 (2D 29)
Church La. SP2: Sal 1A 28
  SP4: Ame 5G 13
  SP4: Bul 6B 10
  SP5: Bis 4A 32
  SP5: Brit 6A 30
  SP5: Pit 5C 24
  SP9: Tid 6G 3
  SP11: Lud 1D 4
  (off High St.)
Church Leat SP5: Dow 1C 38
Church Pk. SP4: Dur 4H 9
Church Rd. SP1: Ford, Lav 1H 29
  SP4: Brig, Mil 2A 10
Church St. SP4: Ame 5G 13
  SP4: Dur 4H 9
  SP6: Fordi 6E 41
Clarence Cl. SP11: Lud 1D 4
Clarence Ct. SP1: Sal 3C 42 (2F 29)
Clarendon Centre, The SP1: Sal 4H 29
  (off Dairy Mdw. La.)
Clarendon Ct. SP9: Tid 4G 3
Clarendon Rd. SP1: Sal 2G 29
  SP5: Alderb 5B 30
  SP5: Alderb, W Gri 2F 37
Clayton Rd. SP4: Bul 6C 10
Clearbury Cl. SP5: Ods 4F 35
Clearbury Vw. SP5: Dow 2A 38
Cleveland Flats SP1: Sal 2G 29
Clifton Rd. SP2: Sal 1D 28

Clifton Row SP2: Sal 2D 28
  (off West St.)
Cloisters, The SP4: Ame 4H 13
  (off London Rd.)
Close, The SP1: Sal 6B 42 (3E 29)
  SP4: Old S 1H 21
  SP5: Mor V 2G 39
Clough La. SP5: Midd W 2H 25
Clover Gdns. SP11: Lud 1E 5
Clover La. SP4: Dur 4G 9
Club Ga. SP9: Tid 6F 3
Club Rd. SP4: Bul C 5G 11
Coach Ho. M. SP4: Ame 5H 13
Cobb La. SP5: W Win 2F 25
Cockey Down Nature Reserve 5B 22
Cocks Cl. SP4: Lark 5B 8
Cold Harbour SP4: Ame 4H 13
Coldharbour La. SP2: Sal 1D 28
College Rd. SP4: Dur 4H 9
College Rdbt. SP1: Sal 6D 42 (4F 29)
College St. SP1: Sal 1D 42 (1F 29)
Collingbourne Rd. SP9: Tid 1F 3
Collingwood Cl. SP5: Whad 3H 37
Collins Cl. SP9: Tid 3F 3
Collis Ter. SP11: Lud 1E 5
Colquhoun Rd. SP4: Lark 6E 9
Coltsfoot Cl. SP4: Ame 5A 14
COMMON, THE 6H 25
Common, The SP5: Midd W 6H 25
Common Va. SP5: Midd W 6G 25
Compton Rd. SP9: Tid 5G 3
Congreve Rd. SP4: Lark 5B 8
Coniston Cl. SP4: Ame 5C 14
Connaught Rd. SP9: Tid 5G 3
Constable Way SP2: Sal 1C 28
Conyger Rd. SP4: Ame 6A 14
Cooks Cl. SP2: Sal 4H 19
Coolins, The SP2: Quid 6F 19
COOMBE BISSETT 4F 33
Coombe Nurseries Caravan Pk.
  SP2: N'ton 6D 26
Coombe Rd. SP2: Sal 6C 28
Coopers Cl. SP4: Ame 4H 13
Copse, The SP5: Alderb 3F 37
Cornflower Way SP11: Lud 2E 5
Cornwall Rd. SP1: Sal 6E 21
Coronation Rd. SP2: Sal 6B 20
  SP4: Dur 5H 9
  SP9: Tid 3F 3
  SP11: Lud 1F 5
Coronation Sq. SP2: Quid 6F 19
Coronation Ter. SP6: San 4A 40
Coronation Villa SP4: N'avon 1F 7
Cottage M. SP6: Fordi 4E 41
Cottages, The SP2: Sal 4D 28
COUNTESS 3G 13
Countess Ct. SP4: Ame 4G 13
Countess Rd. SP4: Ame, Lark 6G 9
COUNTESS SERVICE AREA 3G 13
Court Farm Cl. SP4: N'avon 1F 7
Court Farm Rd. SP4: N'avon 2F 7
Courtwood Cl. SP1: Sal 3G 29
  (off Shady Bower)
Cow La. SP1: Sal 1G 29
  SP11: Kim 5E 5
Cranborne Ct. SP4: Bul C 5G 11
Cranbury Cl. SP5: Dow 3C 38
Crane Bri. Rd. SP2: Sal 4A 42 (3E 29)
Crane Lodge SP2: Sal 4A 42 (3E 29)
Crane St. SP1: Sal 4A 42 (3E 29)
Cranleigh Cl. SP4: Ame 5C 14
Crawlboys La. SP11: Lud 1G 5
Crawlboys Rd. SP11: Lud 1G 5
Crescent, The SP1: Sal 3D 42 (2F 29)
  SP2: Sal 6F 29
  SP2: Wilt 1B 26
  SP4: Ame 4B 14
  SP4: Bul C 5H 11
  SP4: Old S 1H 21
Crescent Rd. SP4: Bul 1B 14
Crestmount Dr. SP4: Ame 6A 20
CRIDDLESTYLE 5H 41
Croft, The SP2: Sal 2B 28
  SP4: Brig 2A 10
Cross Keys Chequer SP1: Sal 3C 42 (2F 29)
Cross Stones SP4: Dur 4H 9
Crossways Cl. SP5: Dow 1E 39
Crow La. SP2: Wilt 6D 18
Crown Cl. SP2: Sal 6B 20
Crown Court
  Salisbury 5C 42 (3E 29)

Crown Ho. SP11: Lud 1E 5
Crown La. SP11: Lud 1D 4
Crown Vs. SP11: Lud 1D 4
　　　　　　　　　　　　　　　(off Crown La.)
Crusades, The SP1: Sal 4G 21
Culver St. SP1: Sal 4D 42 (3F 29)
　　　　　　　　　　　　　　(not continuous)
Cunningham Ho. SP9: Tid 3F 3
　　　　　　　　(off Sidbury Circular Rd.)
Cursus, The . . . . .1A 12 & 6D 12
Cygnet Dr. SP4: Dur 5A 10

D

Dairy Cl. SP5: Woodf 4G 39
Dairyhouse Bri. Caravan Site SP1: Sal . .4H 29
Dairy Mdw. La. SP1: Sal 4H 29
Dalewood Ri. SP1: Lav 1A 30
Darrell Rd. SP4: Ame 4A 14
Darwin Cl. SP4: Bul C 6G 11
Dasna Rd. SP9: Tid 6E 3
Daunch Cl. SP9: Tid 4E 3
David Hart Bus. Cen. SP5: Dow 1B 38
David's Gdn. SP5: Pit 6C 24
Dawbeney Dr. SP4: Ame 5B 14
Deacon Rd. SP11: Kim, Lit S 6H 5
Deans Cl. SP9: Tid 6G 3
Denison Ri. SP1: Sal 5G 21
Denton Dr. SP4: Ame 6A 14
De Vaux Pl. SP1: Sal 6B 42 (4E 29)
Devereux Rd. SP4: Ame 4G 3
Devizes Ho. SP9: Tid 4A 20
Devizes Rd. SP2: Sal 3H 19
　　SP3: 3H 19
Devonshire Rd. SP1: Sal 6E 21
Deweys La. SP11: Lud 1E 5
Dew's Rd. SP2: Sal 2D 28
Diamond Cl. SP6: Fordi 6E 41
Diamond Ct. SP6: Fordi 6E 41
Dickinson Ho. SP9: Tid 6G 3
Diddledown Rd. SP4: Ame 6A 14
DITCHAMPTON 4H 29
Dolphin Ind. Est. SP1: Sal 4H 29
Dolphin St. SP1: Sal 5D 42 (3F 29)
Donaldson Rd. SP1: Sal 1E 29
Dorset Cl. SP4: Bul 6C 10
Dorset Rd. SP1: Sal 6F 21
Double Hedges SP4: Bul 1C 14
Douglas Brown's Wlk. SP4: Lark 6B 8
Douglas Haig Rd. SP1: Sal 6E 21
Down Barn Cl. SP4: Wint G 3D 16
Down Barn Rd. SP4: Wint G 1A 16
Downlands Cl. SP5: Dow 3C 38
Downland Way SP4: Dur 5G 9
Downleaze SP4: Dur 4H 9
Downside SP2: Wilt 1B 26
Downside Rd. SP4: N'avon 1E 7
Downs Vw. Cl. SP4: Hax 1F 7
Downsview Way SP11: Per D 5C 4
Downsway SP1: Sal 5F 21
DOWNTON 2D 38
Downton Bus. Cen. SP5: Dow 1B 38
Downton Hill SP5: Mor V 2F 39
Downton Leisure Cen. 1A 38
Downton Rd. SP2: Sal 5F 29
Down Vw. Rd. SP1: Lav 1A 30
Downwood Cl. SP6: Fordi 4D 40
Drake Cl. SP1: Sal 4G 21
Drove, The SP4: Ame 4H 13
　　SP5: Mor V 3G 39
　　SP5: Woodf 4G 39
Drove Cl. SP5: Coombe B 3F 33
Drove La. SP5: Coombe B 6E 27
Drovers Vw. SP11: Lud 2D 4
Drummer La. SP9: Tid 6G 3
Dryden Cl. SP2: Sal 1H 29
Duck La. SP1: Lav 3F 41
Dudley Av. SP6: Fordi 6C 10
Dukes Way SP4: Bul 6C 10
Dunford Cl. SP4: Ame 5H 15
Dunley Way SP1: Sal 4G 21
DURRINGTON 5H 9
Durrington Swimming & Fitness Cen. 4A 10

E

Eagle Fld. SP2: Sal 5B 20
Earls Cl. SP4: Ame 6C 14
Earls Ct. Rd. SP4: Ame 5H 13

Earls Mnr. Ct. SP4: Wint E 5C 16
EAST GOMELDON 4H 17
E. Gomeldon Rd. SP4: Gom 3E 17
Eastman Cl. SP5: Dow 3D 38
Easton Comn. Hill SP5: Midd W 6H 25
East St. SP2: Sal 3A 42 (2D 28)
Ebble Cl. SP9: Tid 4G 3
Ebbleside Vs. SP1: Nun 4H 35
Edelweiss Cl. SP11: Lud 2E 5
Edgam Pl. SP2: Quid 6F 19
Edison Rd. SP2: Sal 3C 28
Edwards Rd. SP4: Ame 5H 13
Elden Rd. SP9: Tid 5E 3
Eleanor Ct. SP11: Lud 1D 4
Elizabeth Cl. SP5: Dow 2A 38
Elizabeth Cl. SP4: Sal 4A 42 (2E 29)
Elizabeth Rd. SP2: Wilt 4B 18
　　SP4: Dur 5H 9
Elizabeth Sq. SP9: Tid 4H 3
Elliott Grn. SP4: Wint G 4E 17
Elm Cl. SP1: Lav 5C 24
　　SP5: Pit 1G 5
　　SP11: Lud 1E 5
Elm Ct. SP1: Sal 3D 42 (2F 29)
Elmfield SP5: Woodf 4G 39
Elm Gro. SP1: Sal 2G 29
Elm Gro. Pl. SP1: Sal 2G 29
　　　　　　　　　　　　　　　(off Elm Gro.)
Elm Gro. Rd. SP1: Sal 3D 42 (2F 29)
Elms Cl. SP6: San 4A 40
Elmwood Av. SP6: Fordi 4C 40
Empire Rd. SP2: Sal 1A 28
Empress Way SP11: Lud 1D 4
Endle Ct. SP1: Sal 2C 42 (2F 29)
Endless St. SP1: Sal 2B 42 (2E 29)
Equinox Dr. SP4: Ame 3C 14
Essex Sq. SP2: Sal 5B 28
Estcourt Rd. SP1: Sal 2D 42 (2F 29)
Eveque Ct. SP2: Quid 6F 19
Evergreen Way SP4: Ame 6A 14
Everleigh Rd. SP4: Hax 1F 7
Exeter St. SP1: Sal 6C 42 (4F 29)
Exeter St. Rdbt. SP1: Sal 6C 42 (4F 29)
Eyres Dr. SP5: Alderb 3G 37
Eyres Way SP1: Sal 5D 42 (3F 29)

F

FABERSTOWN .1G 5
Fairfax Cl. SP4: Ame 4G 13
Fairfield Rd. SP1: Sal 5E 21
Fairgate Centre, The SP6: Bur 2G 41
Fairings, The SP6: Fordi 5F 41
　　　　　　　　　　　　　　(off Market Pl.)
Fair Vw. Rd. SP2: Wilt 5E 19
Fairview Rd. SP1: Sal 2G 29
Falconsway SP2: Sal 6E 29
Falconwood Cl. SP6: Fordi 5D 40
Faraday Cen. SP2: Sal 2C 28
Fargo Rd. SP4: Lark 1F 13
Fargo Cl. SP4: Lark 6A 8
Fargo Rd. SP4: Lark 4G 29
Farley Rd. SP1: Sal 4G 29
Farm La. SP2: Sal 2C 28
Farm La. Bus. Cen. SP2: Sal 2C 28
Farriers SP6: Fordi 5F 41
Faulston Drove SP5: Bis 5A 32
Ferndown Ct. SP6: Fordi 5D 40
Festival Av. SP2: Sal 6E 21
Feversham Rd. SP1: Sal 5G 7
FIGHELDEAN 5E 17
Figsbury Ridge SP4: Wint G 5E 17
Figsbury Rd. SP4: Wint D 6D 16
Finches Ct. SP1: Sal 3C 42 (2F 29)
Finchley Rd. SP2: Sal 2C 28
Finnis Rd. SP4: Ame 5H 13
Firs Cl. SP5: Firs 2C 24
FIRSDOWN 3G 37
Firs Rd. SP5: Alderb 1A 24
　　SP5: Firs 2A 18
First Broad Dr. SP2: Bar St M 1G 27
Fishermans Reach SP2: Quid 5H 41
Fishers Heron SP6: Fordi 2D 28
Fisherton Island SP2: Sal 2D 28
Fisherton Mill Galleries 3A 42 (2D 28)
Fisherton St. SP2: Sal 3A 42 (2D 28)
Fish Row SP1: Sal 4B 42
Fison Wlk. SP1: Sal 5H 21
FITTLETON 1F 7
Fitzgibbon Sq. SP4: Lark 6B 8

Fitz Gilbert Ct. SP11: Lud 1C 4
Five Rivers Indoor Bowls Club 3G 29
Five Rivers Leisure Centre & Swimming Pool
　　　　　　　　　　　　　　　　　　　.6D 20
Flashett, The SP5: Midd W 6H 25
Flaxfields End SP6: Fordi 5E 41
Fleming Cl. SP11: Lud 1E 5
Flitcroft SP4: Ame 6A 14
Flood, The SP5: Midd W 2H 25
Florence Ct. SP2: Wilt 6C 18
Florence M. SP2: Wilt 6C 18
Flower La. SP4: Ame 5D 28
Folkestone Rd. SP2: Sal 6D 28
Folly Cl. SP2: Sal 1B 28
Folly La. SP2: Sal 2E 37
　　SP5: Alderb 4A 20
Folly Vw. SP2: Sal 6G 19
Foot's Hill SP2: Quid 3A 22
FORD 4G 39
Forder's Cl. SP5: Woodf 5F 41
FORDINGBRIDGE 5F 41
Fordingbridge Bus. Pk. SP6: Fordi 5C 40
FORDINGBRIDGE HOSPITAL 5F 41
Fordingbridge Mus. 5F 41
Fordingbridge Rd. SP6: Alderh, Fordi 6B 40
Forest Ct. SP6: Fordi 5F 41
　　SP9: Tid 4H 3
Forest Dr. SP9: Tid 5H 3
Forest Edge SP5: Dow 5C 38
Forest Rd. SP5: Woodf 5G 39
　　SP6: Hale 3A 22
Fosters Bushes SP4: Ame 5B 14
Foster Wlk. SP4: Lark 5E 9
Fotherby Cres. SP1: Sal 5G 21
Foundary Rd. SP5: Mor V 2G 39
Fountain Way SP2: Sal 2C 28
Fowler's Hill SP1: Sal 3G 29
Fowler's Rd. SP1: Sal 4D 42 (3G 29)
Foxmore Drove SP2: N'ton 6H 27
　　SP5: Coombe B, N'ton 6H 27
Foxtail Gdns. SP11: Lud 1E 5
Francis Cl. SP2: Sal 2A 42
Francis Way SP2: Sal 6E 29
Freemantle Rd. SP11: Per D 4C 4
Friars Orchard SP1: Sal 5C 42 (3F 29)
Friary, The SP1: Sal 6C 42
　　　　　　　　　　　　　　　　　(St Ann St.)
　　SP1: Sal 6C 42
　　　　　　　　　　　　　　　(Whitefriars Rd.)
Friary La. SP1: Sal 6C 42 (4F 29)
Frog La. SP6: Fordi 6E 41
Fryern Ct. Rd. SP6: Bur 2E 41
Fugglestone SP2: Wilt 6E 19
FUGGLESTONE ST PETER 5F 19
Furze Dr. SP11: Per D 5C 4
Furze Hill Rd. SP9: Tid 6G 3
Fyfield Cl. SP1: Sal 4H 21
Fyfield Way SP11: Per D 5C 4

G

Gainsborough Cl. SP2: Sal 6A 20
Gala Bingo
　　Salisbury 3B 42 (2E 29)
Gallipoli Rd. SP4: Bul C 6H 11
Gardiner Rd. SP4: Lark 6B 8
Garendon Ct. SP6: Fordi 4E 41
Gas La. SP2: Sal 1D 28
Gason Hill Rd. SP9: Tid 3F 3
Gaters La. SP4: Wint D 5C 16
Gauntlet Rd. SP4: Ame 4H 13
Gawthorne Dr. SP2: Sal 5D 28
Gaza Rd. SP4: Bul C 5G 11
Geneville Ri. SP4: Ame 5A 14
George VI Rd. SP9: Tid 3F 3
George St. SP1: Sal 1A 42 (1D 28)
George St. Sth. SP2: Sal 2A 42 (2D 28)
Gerard Ho. SP2: Sal 5D 28
　　　　　　　　　　　　　　　(off Hollows Cl.)
Gibbs Cl. SP1: Sal 6G 21
Gigant St. SP1: Sal 4C 42 (3F 29)
Gilbert Way SP1: Sal 5G 21
Glebe Ct. SP5: Pit 5C 24
Glebe Rd. SP4: Dur 4H 9
Glencourt SP2: Sal 6G 21
Glendale Cres. SP1: Sal 3H 29
Glendale Rd. SP4: Dur 5A 10
Glenfield Cl. SP5: Midd W 6H 25
Glenmore Bus. Pk. SP2: Sal 3C 28
Glenmore Rd. SP1: Sal 6G 21

Glenside Gdns. SP1: Sal 3G 29
Glover Rd. SP4: Lark 4D 8
Glyndebourne Cl. SP2: Sal 6A 20
Godley Rd. SP2: Sal 5E 29
Goggs La. SP5: Red 3H 39
GOMELDON 3E 17
Gomeldon Rd. SP4: Gom, Por, Wint G 4E 17
Goodbody Rd. SP4: Lark 6E 9
Gore Rd. SP4: Lark 5B 8
Gorringe Rd. SP2: Sal 2B 28
Gould Cl. SP11: Lud 1D 4
Grace Cl. SP2: Sal 4H 19
Graham Ho. SP1: Sal 4D 42
Graham Sq. SP4: Lark 6B 8
Gramshaw Rd. SP2: Sal 1B 28
Grand Trunk Rd. SP9: Tid . . . . . .6C 2 & 6E 3
Grange Gdns. SP1: Sal 1G 29
Grasmere Cl. SP2: Sal 5D 28
Graspan Rd. SP11: Fab 2G 5
Gravel Cl. SP5: Dow 1B 38
Great Cft. SP5: Firs 2C 24
Great Drove SP4: Wint E 5B 16
GREAT SHODDESDEN 5G 5
Green, The SP1: Lav 1H 29
  SP5: Alderb 2E 37
  SP5: Pit 6C 24
Greenacres SP5: Dow 1A 38
Greencroft SP1: Sal 3D 42
Greencroft St. SP1: Sal 2C 42 (2F 29)
Greenlands Cl. SP4: Dur 5H 9
Green La. SP1: Ford 3H 21
  SP2: Sal 6C 28
  SP4: Ford, Old S 1H 21
  SP5: Dow 1C 38
  SP6: Fordi 4F 41
                                              (Picket Cl.)
  SP6: Fordi 1D 40
                                          (Whitsbury Rd.)
Greenlane Dr. SP4: Ford 3H 21
Greens Ct. SP1: Sal 5C 42 (3F 29)
Greens Meade SP5: Woodf 3G 39
Greenwood Av. SP1: Lav 2H 29
Gregory Ct. SP2: Sal 2A 42
Greyfriars Cl. SP1: Sal 6C 42 (4F 29)
Greyhound La. SP2: Wilt 6D 18
                                      (off Kingsbury Sq.)
Griffins Ct. SP2: Sal 3A 42 (2E 29)
Grimstead Rd. SP5: W Gri, Whad 4H 37
                                            (not continuous)
Grosvenor Cl. SP9: Tid 5H 3
Grosvenor Ct. SP2: Sal 2D 28
Grouse Rd. SP4: Old S 1F 21
Grove La. SP5: Red 2H 39
Grovely Vw. SP2: Wilt 2B 26
Guilder Centre, The 3C 42
Guilder La. SP1: Sal 3D 42 (3F 29)
Guildhall Sq. SP1: Sal 3B 42
Gunner St. SP4: Bul C 1E 15
Gunville Hill SP5: Midd W 6H 25
Gunville Rd. SP5: Midd W 6H 25
Gypsy La. SP1: Pet 3A 30
  SP5: Coombe B 6F 33
  SP5: Pet 3A 30

H

Hackthorne Rd. SP4: Dur 3G 9
Hadleigh Ct. SP1: Sal 3G 29
Hadrians Ct. SP2: Sal 2A 28
Haig Rd. SP4: Bul C 6E 11
HALE 6G 39
Hale La. SP6: Hale 6D 38
Hales Rd. SP4: N'avon 1E 7
Halfpenny Rd. SP2: Sal 4B 28
Hallum Cl. SP1: Sal 5H 21
Halton Rd. SP11: Per D 4C 4
Ham, The SP4: Dur 4H 9
Hambrook Ct. SP4: Ame 5H 15
Hamilton Cl. SP4: Ame 5B 14
Hamilton Cl. SP9: Tid 6F 3
Hamilton Grn. SP9: Tid 6F 3
Hamilton Pk. SP5: Dow 1D 38
Hamilton Rd. SP1: Sal 1B 42 (1E 29)
Hampshire Cl. SP4: Bul 6C 10
Hampshire Cross SP9: Tid 5G 3
Hampton Ct. SP2: Quid 6F 19
HAMPTON PARK 4G 21
Haragon Dr. SP4: Ame 5H 15
Harcourt Ter. SP2: Sal 4A 42 (3D 28)
Hardings, The SP2: Sal 2D 28

Hardy Ho. SP2: Sal 3D 28
                                            (off Rectory Rd.)
Harefield Cres. SP4: N'avon 4F 7
Hare Warren Cl. SP2: Wilt 2C 26
HARNHAM 4C 28
Harnham Bus. Pk. SP2: Sal 5A 28
Harnham Gate 6B 42 (4E 29)
Harnham Rd. SP2: Sal 4D 28
Harnham Rdbt. SP2: Sal 5E 29
Harnham Trad. Est. SP2: Sal 4B 28
Harnwood Rd. SP2: Sal 6C 28
Harper Rd. SP2: Sal 1B 28
Harrington Dr. SP4: Bul C 6F 11
Harthill Drove SP5: Red 4H 39
Hartington Rd. SP2: Sal 1D 28
Hartley Way SP1: Sal 4G 21
Harvard Cl. SP2: Sal 6D 28
Harvard Way SP4: Ame 6A 14
                                            (not continuous)
Hatches La. SP1: Sal 4H 29
Hatchet Cl. SP6: Hale 6G 39
HATCHET GREEN 6F 39
Hathaway Cl. SP1: Sal 5D 20
Hawkes Cl. SP4: Ame 6B 14
Hawksridge SP1: Sal 6E 29
Hawthorn Cl. SP2: Sal 2D 28
Hawthorn Rd. SP9: Tid 4H 3
HAXTON 1F 7
Hayters Flats SP2: Sal 3A 42 (2D 28)
Haywain SP4: Ame 5H 13
                                            (not continuous)
Hazel Cl. SP2: Sal 6H 19
Headlands, The SP5: Dow 1B 38
Headquarters Rd. SP4: Bul C 1G 15
Heath Rd. SP2: Sal 5B 20
Heath Sq. SP4: Lark 6B 8
Heath Vw. Dr. SP2: Sal 6A 20
Hedley Davis Ct. SP2: Sal 2B 28
Hei-Lin Way SP11: Lud 1D 4
Helena Ter. SP2: Sal 2D 42
Herbert Rd. SP2: Sal 6A 20
  SP5: Woodf 3G 39
Herman Way SP4: Gom 4F 17
Heronswood SP2: Sal 6E 29
Heron Wlk. SP4: Dur 5A 10
Hertford Cl. SP6: Fordi 3F 41
Heyford Cl. SP4: Ame 5C 14
Highbank Gdns. SP6: Fordi 5F 41
Highbury Av. SP2: Sal 1C 28
Highbury Cl. SP2: Sal 1C 28
Highfield Cres. SP5: Midd W 3H 25
Highfield La. SP5: Woodf 4G 39
Highfield Rd. SP2: Sal 1C 28
  SP4: Ame 5H 13
Highlands Rd. SP2: Sal 5E 29
High Post Rd. SP4: Wint G 4B 16
High Rd. SP5: Brit 6G 29
High St. SP1: Sal 5B 42 (3E 29)
                                            (not continuous)
  SP4: Ame 4G 13
  SP4: Bul 6A 10
  SP4: Dur 4H 9
  SP4: Fig 6G 7
  SP4: N'avon 2F 7
  SP4: Por 2F 17
  SP5: Alderb 2E 37
  SP5: Dow 2D 38
  SP5: Pit 6C 24
  SP6: Fordi 5F 41
  SP11: Lud 1D 4
High Street Gate 4B 42 (3E 29)
Highway, The SP5: Charl S 6B 36
Hillcrest Mobile Home Pk. SP4: Ame 4B 14
Hillcroft SP5: Woodf 3G 39
Hill Rd. SP1: Lav 1A 30
Hillside Dr. SP4: Gom 4F 17
Hillsway Cen. SP4: Ame 4B 14
Hill Top Av. SP9: Tid 3F 3
Hill Top Cl. SP4: Fig 5G 7
Hilltop Way SP1: Sal 4E 21
Hillview Cl. SP4: Ame 4H 13
Hillview Rd. SP1: Sal 3D 42 (2F 29)
Hoadley Grn. SP1: Sal 5H 21
Holders Rd. SP4: Ame 4A 14
Hollies, The SP4: Ford 3A 22
Holloway Cl. SP4: Ame 5H 15
Hollows, The SP2: Wilt 5B 18
Hollows Ct. SP2: Sal 5D 28
Holly Vs. SP6: San 4A 40
Homebridge Ho. SP6: Fordi 4F 41

Home Farm Rd. SP2: N'ton, Wilt 2C 26
HOMINGTON 4A 34
Homington Rd. SP5: Coombe B, Hom 4F 33
                                            (not continuous)
Horefield SP4: Por 1G 17
Horne Rd. SP4: Bul C 5E 11
Horse Barrow SP4: Wint G 4E 17
HORSEPORT 5G 41
Horseshoe Ct. SP5: Dow 1C 38
Howard Vyse Rd. SP4: Lark 5C 8
Hubert Hamilton Rd. SP4: Bul C 6F 11
                                            (not continuous)
Hudson Rd. SP1: Sal 6D 20
  SP4: Ame 4A 14
Hudson's Fld. SP1: Sal 5D 20
Hughenden Mnr. SP5: Pet 4A 30
Hulse Rd. SP1: Sal 1A 42 (1E 29)
Humber La. SP1: Sal 6F 3
Hundred, The SP6: Fordi 5F 41
HURDCOTT 1B 22
Hurdcott La. SP4: Hur, Wint E 1B 22
Hurley Cl. SP4: Ame 5B 14
Hurricane Cl. SP4: Old S 1G 21
Hussey's Almshouses SP1: Sal . .2B 42 (2E 29)
Hyde La. SP5: Dow 2A 38
Hynes Ct. SP11: Lud 1D 4
Hyson Cres. SP11: Lud 1G 5

I

Idmiston Rd. SP4: Por 2G 17
Ilynton Av. SP5: Firs 2C 24
Imber Av. SP4: Ame 6B 14
India Av. SP2: Sal 1B 28
Ivy Pl. SP1: Sal 2B 42 (2E 29)
Ivy St. SP1: Sal 4C 42 (3F 29)

J

Jaggard Vw. SP4: Ame 5A 14
James Rd. SP4: Ame 4A 14
James St. SP2: Sal 2D 28
Jamrud Rd. SP9: Tid 6E 3
Javelin Cl. SP4: Ame 5B 14
Jewell Cl. SP1: Sal 5H 21
Joanna Cl. SP5: Dow 2A 38
John French Way SP4: Bul 6C 10
John Gay Rd. SP4: Ame 5H 13
Johnson Way SP11: Lud 2D 4
John Wood Ho. SP2: Sal 4A 42 (3E 29)
Joseph Ct. SP2: Sal 2A 42
Jubilee Cl. SP2: Sal 6A 20
  SP6: Fordi 5C 40
Jubilee Ct. SP2: Sal 1D 28
                                            (off Meadow Rd.)
  SP2: Sal 3A 42
                                                  (North St.)
  SP9: Tid 4G 3
Jubilee Cres. SP6: Fordi 5D 40
Jubilee Rd. SP6: Fordi 5C 40
Julius Ct. SP2: Sal 2A 42
Junction Rd. SP5: Alderb 2F 37
Juniper Ct. SP9: Tid 4H 3
Juniper Dr. SP1: Sal 4E 21
Juniper Rd. SP5: Firs 2C 24

K

Kandy Rd. SP4: Bul C 6F 11
Karachi Cl. SP9: Tid 4F 3
Kashmir Rd. SP4: Bul C 6E 11
Keel Cl. SP4: Ame 6A 14
Kelsey Rd. SP1: Sal 3D 42 (2F 29)
Kemmel Rd. SP11: Per D 4B 4
Kennel Row SP4: N'avon 2F 7
Kennet Rd. SP9: Tid 4G 3
Kensington Rd. SP2: Sal 1D 28
Kent Rd. SP2: Sal 5C 28
Kerby Av. SP4: N'avon 2G 7
Kerry Gdns. SP6: San 4B 40
Kickdom Cl. SP4: Ame 6B 14
Kilford Cl. SP4: Ame 5G 15
Kiln Cl. SP5: Whad 4H 37
Kiln Rd. SP5: Red 2H 39
Kimber Cl. SP9: Tid 4F 3
Kimpton Av. SP1: Sal 4H 21
Kingfisher Cl. SP2: Sal 6E 29
Kingfisher Dr. SP4: Dur 5A 10

Kingsbourne Cl. SP4: Wint D 6D 16
Kingsbury Sq. SP2: Wilt 6D 18
Kings Ct. SP6: Fordi 5F 41
Kingsford Cl. SP5: Woodf 4G 39
Kings Ga. SP2: Wilt 5E 19
Kings Hill SP4: N'avon 2F 7
Kingsland Rd. SP2: Wilt 1D 28
Kings Paddock SP5: W Win 4G 25
Kings Rd. SP1: Sal 1B 42 (1E 29)
King St. SP2: Wilt .5D 18
Kingsway SP2: Wilt 5E 19
Kingsway Bus. Cen. SP2: Wilt 5D 18
Kings Yd. SP6: Fordi 5F 41
(off Salisbury St.)
Kirkee Rd. SP9: Tid .6F 3
Kitchener Rd. SP4: Ame 4H 13
Kivel Ct. SP2: Sal 1A 42 (1E 29)
Kiwi Rd. SP4: Bul C 5H 11
Knights Cl. SP5: Midd W 2H 25
Kohat Cl. SP9: Tid 4E 3
Kohat Rd. SP9: Tid .6F 3

L

Lady Diana Ct. SP11: Lud 1E 5
Lady Godley Cl. SP9: Tid 6F 3
Lady Jane Wlk. SP11: Lud 1E 5
Ladysmith SP4: Gom 4F 17
Ladysmith Ct. SP4: Gom 4F 17
Ladysmith Rd. SP2: Sal 6B 20
Ladyway SP4: Idm 1H 17
LA Fitness
Salisbury 3A 42 (2D 28)
Lahore Cl. SP9: Tid .4F 3
Lahore Rd. SP9: Tid .6F 3
Lambdown App. SP11: Per D 5B 4
Lambdown Ter. SP11: Per D 5A 4
Lampard Ter. SP2: Wilt 1C 26
Lancaster Rd. SP4: Old S 2G 21
Lane, The SP4: Por 1F 17
Lane's Cl. SP4: Ame 4A 14
Lanfear Cl. SP4: Ame 4A 14
Lanfranc Cl. SP4: Old S 2F 21
Langford La. SP5: Dow, Red 1G 39
Langley Gdn. SP6: Fordi 3G 41
LARKHILL 5B 8
Larkhill Racecourse 6B 6
Larkhill Rd. SP4: Dur 5G 9
LAVERSTOCK 2H 29
Laverstock & Ford Sports Club 6H 21
Laverstock Pk. SP1: Lav 1H 29
Laverstock Pk. W. SP1: Lav 1H 29
Laverstock Rd. SP1: Sal 3G 29
Law Courts
Salisbury 1C 28
Lawrence Cl. SP4: Ame 6A 14
Lawrence Grn. SP2: Sal 1D 28
(off Ashley Rd.)
Lawrence Rd. SP4: Lark 5C 8
Lawson Rd. SP4: Lark 6E 9
Leaze, The SP4: Bul 6C 10
Ledger Hill Cl. SP4: Bul 6B 10
Lees Ct. SP2: Sal .1D 28
Lena Cl. SP11: Lud .1E 5
Leonard Cheshire Cl. SP4: Ame 6B 14
Levell Ct. SP11: Lud 1E 5
Lightfoot Rd. SP4: Lark 6C 8
Lightning Rd. SP4: Ame 6B 14
Light's La. SP5: Alderb 3E 37
Lily Wlk. SP4: Dur .5A 10
Lime Kiln Way SP2: Sal 6E 29
Limes, The SP4: Por 1G 17
Linden Cl. SP1: Lav 2H 29
SP11: Lud 1F 5
Lindford Rd. SP1: Sal 4H 21
Lindley Cl. SP9: Tid 5G 3
Linkway SP1: Sal .6G 21
Linnetsdene SP2: Sal 6E 29
Lions Ga. SP6: Fordi 5F 41
Little Ann SP4: Wint E 6C 16
LITTLE DURNFORD 1A 20
LITTLE SHODDESDEN 5H 5
Lit. Woodfalls Dr. SP5: Woodf 5G 39
Livery Rd. SP5: Midd W, W Win 4G 25
Lock's La. SP2: Quid 6G 19
Lode Hill SP5: Dow 1D 38
Lode Hill Caravan Site SP5: Dow 1E 39
Lodge Drove SP5: Woodf 5F 39
Londonderry Gdns. SP4: Bul C 5E 11

London Rd. SP1: Sal 1G 29
SP4: Ame 4H 13
SP5: Firs 1A 24
London Road (Park & Ride) 5H 21
Long Cl. SP5: Dow 1B 38
Long Cl. West SP5: Dow 1B 38
Longfield Cl. SP4: Dur 5G 9
Longhill Dr. SP2: Sal 6F 29
Longland SP2: Sal 2C 28
Lords Cft. SP4: Ame 4H 13
Love La. SP1: Sal 5C 42 (3F 29)
Lovett Grn. SP1: Sal 5G 21
Lowa Rd. SP9: Tid 5F 3
Lower Bartons SP6: Fordi 5F 41
LOWER BURGATE 2G 41
Lower Folly SP2: Wilt 2B 26
Lower Rd. SP2: Quid, Sal 6F 19
SP4: N'avon 2F 7
SP5: Brit 6G 29
SP5: Hom 4A 34
Lower St. SP4: Sal 4C 28
SP4: Hax 1F 7
LUDGERSHALL 1E 5
Ludgershall Bus. Pk. SP11: Lud 2D 4
Ludgershall Rd. SP9: Tid 4G 3
Lumley Cl. SP2: Sal 4H 19
Lumley Wlk. SP4: Ame 5B 14
Lynchets Rd. SP4: Ame 5H 13
Lynchfield Rd. SP4: Ame 5H 13
Lyndhurst Rd. SP4: Ame 5A 14
Lysander Way SP4: Old S 1G 21
Lyster Rd. SP6: Fordi 4G 41

M

McKie Rd. SP4: Ame 6B 14
Macklin Rd. SP2: Lark 1C 28
McNeill Rd. SP4: Lark 5D 8
McQueen Wlk. SP4: Lark 5E 9
Magdalene Ct. SP1: Sal 4C 42
Main Rd. SP4: Ame 6B 14
SP4: Wint D, Wint E, Wint G 1C 22
Mall, The SP9: Tid 6C 2
Mallard Cl. SP2: Sal 4D 28
Malmesbury Ho. SP9: Tid 5H 3
(off Kennet Rd.)
Malthouse La. SP2: Sal 3A 42 (2E 29)
Malthouse Wlk. SP11: Lud 1D 4
(off Tidsworth Rd.)
Maltings, The SP1: Sal 3A 42 (2E 29)
(not continuous)
Malverns, The SP2: Sal 1B 28
Malvern Way SP4: Por 1F 17
Manning Cl. SP1: Sal 4G 21
Manor Bri. Ct. SP9: Tid 4G 3
Manor Cl. SP6: Fordi 5F 41
Manor Ct. SP1: Sal 1G 29
Manor Farm SP5: Bis 3A 32
Mnr. Farm Rd. SP1: Sal 2G 29
SP4: Ford 2H 21
SP6: Fordi 4C 40
Manor Gdn. SP4: Dur 4H 9
Manor Rd. SP1: Sal 2G 29
Maple Cres. SP2: Wilt 6F 19
SP11: Lud 1G 5
Maplecroft SP2: Sal 6E 29
Maple Dr. SP5: Firs 2C 24
Maple Way SP4: Ame 4B 14
SP4: Dur 4G 9
Marbrean Cl. SP6: Fordi 4C 40
Marchment Cl. SP2: Wilt 5F 19
Margaret's Cl. SP4: Ame 6A 14
Margha Rd. SP9: Tid 5F 3
Marie Av. SP5: Dow 2A 38
Marina Cl. SP4: Dur 5H 9
Marina Cres. SP4: Dur 5G 9
Marina Rd. SP1: Sal 3G 29
SP4: Dur 5G 9
Market Pl. SP2: Wilt 6D 18
(off North St.)
SP6: Fordi 5F 41
Market Wlk. SP1: Sal 3B 42 (2E 29)
Marlborough Rd. SP1: Sal 1C 42 (1E 29)
SP4: Bul C 1F 15
Marl La. SP6: Fordi, San 3C 40
Marne Cres. SP4: Bul C 5F 11
Marne Rd. SP4: Bul C 5F 11
Marsh La. SP4: Sal 1D 28
SP5: Coombe B 3F 33
Marshmead Cl. SP5: Alderb 5B 30

Martinbushes Rd. SP4: Dur 4F 9
Martins Cl. SP2: Sal 6E 29
Martlesham Rd. SP4: Ame 6B 14
Maryland Cl. SP4: Ame 4H 19
Matrons Cotts. SP5: Whad 3H 37
Mayfair Rd. SP1: Lav 2H 29
Mayfield Rd. SP6: Fordi 4C 40
Mayfly Cl. SP6: Fordi 4F 41
Meadens La. SP5: Coombe B 4G 33
Meade Rd. SP11: Lud 1F 5
Meadow Av. SP6: Fordi 4E 41
Meadow Cl. SP6: Fordi 4E 41
Meadow Ct. SP6: Fordi 4F 41
Meadow Rd. SP2: Sal 2A 42 (1D 28)
SP4: Bul 6C 10
Meadow Rd. Sth.
SP2: Sal 2A 42 (2D 28)
Meadows, The SP1: Sal 3H 29
Meadow Vw. SP4: Hax 1F 7
Meadowview Cl. SP11: Per D 5C 4
Meads Rd. SP4: Dur 5H 9
Mears Rd. SP4: Lark 6E 9
Medieval Hall, The 5A 42 (3E 29)
Meerut Rd. SP9: Tid .5F 3
Melbourne Gdns. SP4: Bul C 6G 11
Melor Vw. SP4: Ame 6A 14
Melvin Cl. SP1: Lav 2H 29
Meridian Way SP4: Ame 4C 14
Merom Row SP2: Sal 1D 28
(off Gas La.)
Merrifield Rd. SP4: Ford 3G 21
Merton Cl. SP6: Fordi 3F 41
Mesh Pond SP5: Dow 1A 38
Methuen Dr. SP1: Sal 4D 42 (3G 29)
Meyrick Av. SP2: Sal 5E 29
Middle St. SP2: Sal 4C 28
Middleton SP5: Midd W 3H 25
Middleton Rd. SP2: Sal 1A 42 (1D 28)
SP5: Midd W 2H 25
MIDDLE WINTERSLOW 3H 25
Midgham Rd. SP6: Fordi 6C 40
Mid Summer Pl. SP4: Ame 3B 14
MILFORD 3H 29
Milford Hill SP1: Sal 4D 42 (3F 29)
Milford Hollow SP1: Sal 3G 29
Milford Ind. Est. SP1: Sal 3G 29
Milford Mnr. Gdns. SP1: Sal 3H 29
Milford Mill Rd. SP1: Sal 3H 29
Milford Pk. SP1: Sal 3H 29
Milford St. SP1: Sal 4C 42 (3F 29)
Millbrook SP1: Sal .2G 29
Mill Cl. SP4: Wint G 3D 16
Mill Corner SP4: Wint G 3D 16
Mill Ct. SP6: Fordi .5E 41
Millennium Cl. SP2: Sal 6F 29
Miller Cl. SP1: Strat C 4C 20
Millgreen Rd. SP4: Ame 6A 14
Mill Hill Av. SP9: Tid 3F 3
Mill La. SP1: Strat C 4B 20
SP5: Bis 4A 32
SP5: Midd W, E Win 5H 25
Mill Path SP9: Tid 3E 3
Mill Race Cl. SP2: Sal 2D 28
(off Mill Rd.)
Mill Race Vw. SP5: Dow 1C 38
Mill Rd. SP2: Sal 4A 42 (2D 28)
SP4: N'avon .1E 7
Mill Rd. M. SP2: Sal 2D 28
Mill Stream App. SP1: Sal 2B 42 (2E 29)
Mills Way SP4: Ame 4B 14
Mills Way Bus. Cen.
SP4: Ame 4B 14
Milne Cres. SP4: Lark 6B 8
Milne Rd. SP4: Bul C 1E 15
MILSTON 3A 10
Milston Drove SP4: Bul, Mil 3B 10
Milston Rd. SP4: Bul 3B 10
Milston Vw. SP4: Dur 4A 10
Milton Rd. SP2: Sal 5F 29
SP4: Ame 6C 14
Minores Rd. SP9: Tid 5H 3
Minster St. SP1: Sal 4B 42 (3E 29)
SP2: Wilt 6D 18
Minton Distribution Pk.
SP4: Ame 4B 14
Mitchell Rd. SP2: Sal 3B 28
Mitchells Cl. SP5: Woodf 3G 39
Moberly Rd. SP1: Sal 6E 21
Model Farm La. SP5: Pit 6C 24
Mompesson House 4A 42
Monks Cl. SP9: Tid 4F 3

Mons Av. SP4: Bul C 6E **11**
Montague Rd. SP2: Sal 5B **28**
Montgomery Gdns. SP2: Sal 1C **28**
Montgomery Ho. *SP9: Tid* 3F **3**
(off Sidbury Circular Rd.)
Monxton Cl. SP1: Sal 4H **21**
Moot Cl. SP5: Dow 3D **38**
Moot Gdns. SP5: Dow 3C **38**
Moot La. SP5: Dow 3C **38**
SP6: Hale, Woodg 6C **38**
Morgan's La. SP4: Wint D 5C **16**
Morgans Ri. Rd. SP5: Mor V 2G **39**
MORGAN'S VALE 2G **39**
Morgans Va. Rd. SP5: Mor V 3G **39**
Moxhams SP6: Fordi 5F **41**
Moyne Gdns. SP4: Ame 5B **14**
Muddyford Rd. SP5: Red 2G **39**
Mulberry Gdns. SP6: Fordi 6E **41**
Munks Cl. SP2: Sal 4C **28**
Myrrfield Rd. SP1: Sal 4H **21**

N

Nadder La. SP2: Quid 1F **27**
Nadder Rd. SP9: Tid 5G **3**
Nadder Ter. SP2: Sal 2C **28**
SP2: Wilt 1C **26**
Nahalsen Cl. SP4: Por 1F **17**
Naini Tal Rd. SP9: Tid 5F **3**
Napier Cres. SP1: Lav 2H **29**
Natanbury SP5: Dow 2C **38**
Neal Cl. SP1: Sal 4G **21**
Nelson Cl. SP4: Bul C 6H **11**
Nelson Rd. SP1: Sal 1A **42** (1E **29**)
Nepaul Rd. SP9: Tid 4F **3**
NETHERAVON 2F **7**
Netheravon Cl. SP1: Sal 6F **21**
Netheravon Dovecote 3F **7**
Netheravon Rd. SP1: Sal 1F **29**
SP4: Dur 5G **9**
SP4: Fig 6G **7**
NETHERHAMPTON 3F **27**
Netherhampton Bus. Cen.
SP2: N'ton 3G **27**
Netherhampton Rd.
SP2: N'ton, Quid, Sal 2E **27**
Nevill Cl. SP4: Ame 5H **15**
Neville Cl. SP1: Sal 5G **21**
New Bottom Rd. SP4: Strat C 2C **20**
New Bridge Rd. SP2: Sal 4E **29**
New Brympton Ho. *SP2: Sal* 5D **28**
(off Gawthorne Dr.)
New Canal SP1: Sal 4B **42** (3E **29**)
New Drove SP11: Lud 2D **4**
New Forest National Pk. 6D **38**
New Haig Rd. SP4: Bul C 6E **11**
NEW HALL NHS TREATMENT CENTRE ...5B **36**
(within New Hall Private Hospital)
NEW HALL PRIVATE HOSPITAL 5B **36**
New Harnham Rd. SP2: Sal 5E **29**
Newmans Way SP4: Bul 1C **14**
New Rd. SP4: Dur 5H **9**
New St. SP1: Sal 4B **42** (3E **29**)
Newton Rd. SP2: Sal 2B **28**
Newtown Vs. SP11: Lud 1G **5**
New Ward Rd. SP4: Bul C 6E **11**
New Zealand Av. SP2: Sal 1B **28**
Nicholas Ct. SP2: Sal 2A **42**
Nicolson Cl. SP4: Ame 5C **14**
Nightingale Wlk. *SP2: Sal* 1C **28**
(off Christie Miller Rd.)
Norfolk Rd. SP2: Sal 4B **28**
Normandy Way SP6: Fordi 4E **41**
NORTH CHARFORD
SP6, South Charford 5A **38**
SP6, Woodfalls 5G **39**
Nth. Charford Drove SP6: Bre 5A **38**
Northern Ter. SP4: Lark 5D **8**
Northleigh Ter. SP2: Wilt 6D **18**
North Rd. SP4: Ame 6C **14**
North Rd. Caravan Site SP4: Ame ...6C **14**
Northside SP4: Old S 1H **21**
North St. SP2: Sal 3A **42** (2D **28**)
SP2: Wilt 6D **18**
NORTH TIDWORTH 4F **3**
North Wlk. SP1: Sal 5B **42** (3E **29**)
Norton Dr. SP4: Ford 3H **21**
Norton Enterprise Cen. SP2: Sal ...2B **28**
NUNTON 4H **35**
Nunton Drove SP5: Nun, Ods 6F **35**

Nursery Cl. SP4: Ame 5H **13**
Nursery Rd. SP2: Sal 2C **28**

O

Oak Ash Grn. SP2: Wilt 1C **26**
Oakbournes, The SP1: Sal 4G **21**
Oak Cl. SP9: Tid 4H **3**
Oak Dr. SP5: Alderb 3F **37**
Oaklands Av. SP4: Ame 4B **14**
Oaklands Cl. SP6: Fordi 4E **41**
Oak La. SP4: Fig 5G **7**
Oaklea La. SP5: Whad 3G **37**
Oak Pl. SP4: Ame 3A **14**
Oaktree Field Caravan Site
SP2: Sal 1F **35**
Oakway Rd. SP1: Sal 5F **21**
Oakwood Gro. SP5: Alderb 2F **37**
Oatmeal Row SP1: Sal 3B **42**
Odeon Cinema
Salisbury 4B **42** (3E **29**)
ODSTOCK 4F **35**
Odstock Rd. SP2: Sal 6E **29**
SP5: Sal 6E **29**
Odstock Vw. SP5: Sal 2F **35**
Old Blandford Rd. SP2: Sal 6C **28**
SP5: Coombe B 6D **32**
Old Brewery La. SP4: N'avon 2F **7**
Old Brickyard Rd. SP6: San 4B **40**
Old Castle Rd. SP1: Sal 3E **21**
Old Chapel Cl. SP5: Alderb 2F **37**
Old Coach Rd. SP4: Bul 6B **10**
Old Common Way SP11: Lud 1E **5**
Old Dairy, The SP5: Nun 4H **35**
Old Dairy Cl. SP2: Sal 6A **20**
Oldfield Rd. SP1: Sal 4G **21**
Old George Mall SP1: Sal 4B **42**
Old Granary La. SP4: Ame 5G **13**
Old Malthouse La. SP4: Firs, Ford ..3B **22**
Old Marlborough Rd. SP4: Bul 4F **11**
Old Marlborough Road, The
SP4: Bul, Bul C 4F **11**
Old Meadows Wlk. SP2: Sal 4C **28**
Old Mill Gdns. SP2: Sal 4C **28**
Old Post Office La. SP4: N'avon 2F **7**
Old Rd. SP5: Alderb 1D **36**
OLD SARUM 1F **21**
Old Sarum 3D **20**
Old Sarum Pk. SP4: Old S 1G **21**
Old School Cl. SP4: N'avon 2F **7**
Old Shaftesbury Drove SP2: N'ton, Wilt ..5A **26**
SP5: Coombe B 6A **28**
Old St. SP2: Sal 5E **29**
Old Tannery, The *SP5: Dow* 1D **38**
(off High St.)
Old Vicarage La. SP5: Alderb 4E **37**
Old Vineries, The SP6: Fordi 5D **40**
Old Ward Rd. SP4: Bul C 6D **10**
Olivier Cl. SP2: Sal 4A **20**
Olivier Rd. SP2: Wilt 4B **18**
Orchard, The SP1: Sal 1G **29**
SP5: Nun 4H **35**
Orchard Cl. SP6: Fordi 4F **41**
Orchard End SP4: Bul 6B **10**
Orchard Gdns. SP6: Fordi 5F **41**
Orchard Rd. SP2: Sal 2B **28**
SP5: Mor V 2G **39**
Orchard Way SP4: Ame 5A **14**
Orchid Dr. SP11: Lud 2E **5**
Ordnance Rd. SP9: Tid 5G **3**
Orford Rd. SP4: Ame 6B **14**
Osborne Ho. SP1: Sal 1B **42** (1E **29**)
Osmund Wlk. SP4: Old S 2F **21**
Owlswood SP2: Sal 6E **29**
Ox Drove SP2: Wilt 3A **18**
Ox Row SP1: Sal 4B **42**

P

Paccombe SP5: Red 2G **39**
Packway, The SP4: Lark 5A **8**
Paddock Cl. SP4: Wint D 5D **16**
Paddock Way SP1: Lav 1A **30**
Paddock Wood SP4: Dur 5A **10**
Padstow Pl. SP6: Fordi 6E **41**
Paget Cl. SP9: Tid 3E **3**
Pains Way SP4: Ame 6A **14**
Palmer Rd. SP2: Sal 1C **28**
Pantiles, The SP6: Fordi 5D **40**

Park & Ride
Beehive 2E **21**
Britford 6G **29**
London Road 5H **21**
Petersfinger 4A **30**
Wilton 4E **19**
Park Cl. SP1: Sal 5E **21**
Park Cotts. SP5: Red 2G **39**
Parkers Cl. SP5: Dow 1B **38**
Parkland Way SP4: Por 1F **17**
Park La. SP1: Sal 6E **21**
SP5: Brit 1H **35**
Park Rd. SP1: Lav 1A **30**
SP6: Fordi 4F **41**
Park St. SP1: Sal 1D **42** (1F **29**)
Parkwood Health & Fitness 4A **22**
Parsonage Cl. SP1: Strat C 4C **20**
SP6: Fordi 5F **41**
Parsonage Grn. SP2: Sal 4C **28**
Parsonage Pk. Dr. SP6: Fordi 4E **41**
Parsonage Rd. SP4: Ame 5H **13**
Parsons Cl. SP4: Por 2F **17**
Partridge Way SP4: Old S 1G **21**
Paul's Dene Cres. SP1: Sal 4F **21**
Paul's Dene Rd. SP1: Sal 4E **21**
Paxton Bus. Cen. SP2: Sal 2B **28**
Payne's Hill SP1: Sal 5D **42**
Pealsham Gdns. SP6: Fordi 4E **41**
Pearce Way SP1: Sal 4G **21**
Pembridge Ho. SP6: Fordi 5G **41**
Pembridge Rd. SP6: Fordi 3G **41**
Pembroke Ct. SP2: Wilt 6D **18**
Pembroke Ho. SP2: Sal 4A **42**
Pembroke Rd. SP2: Sal 6A **20**
Penning Rd. SP2: Quid 6G **19**
Pennings, The SP4: Bul C 1D **14**
Pennings Drove SP5: Coombe B 5G **33**
Pennings Rd. SP9: Tid 3F **3**
Pennyfarthing St. SP1: Sal 3C **42** (2F **29**)
Penny La. SP4: Ame 5H **15**
Pennys Cl. SP6: Fordi 3F **41**
Pennys Cres. SP6: Fordi 3F **41**
Pennys La. *SP2: Wilt* 6D **18**
(off Russell St.)
SP6: Fordi 4F **41**
Penruddock Cl. SP2: Sal 6A **20**
Pepperbox Ri. SP5: Whad 3H **37**
Pepy's Wlk. SP1: Sal 4B **42** (3E **29**)
Perham Cres. SP11: Lud 1F **5**
PERHAM DOWN 4C **4**
Perth Rd. SP11: Per D 4C **4**
Peshawar Cl. SP9: Tid 4E **3**
Petersfield Grn. SP9: Tid 5F **3**
PETERSFINGER 4A **30**
Petersfinger (Park & Ride) 4A **30**
Peters Finger Rd. SP5: Pet 4A **30**
Petticoat La. SP5: Red 2H **39**
Pheasant Dr. SP4: Old S 1F **21**
Philip Cl. SP2: Sal 6B **20**
Philip Rd. SP2: Wilt 4B **18**
SP4: Dur 5H **9**
Phillips La. SP1: Strat C 3C **20**
Picket Cl. SP6: Fordi 4F **41**
Pigott Cl. SP4: N'avon 1E **7**
Pilgrims Ct. SP1: Lav 1A **30**
Pilgrims Gate SP1: Lav 1A **30**
Pilgrims Mead SP1: Sal 4G **21**
(not continuous)
Pilgrims Way SP1: Lav 1A **30**
Pilots Vw. SP4: Ame 5B **14**
Pinckneys Way SP4: Dur 5G **9**
Pine Vw. Cl. SP5: Woodf 5G **39**
Pine Wlk. SP4: Ame 5B **14**
Pinewood Cl. SP2: Sal 5H **19**
Pinewood Way SP2: Sal 5H **19**
PITTON 6C **24**
Plantation, The SP5: Midd W 4G **25**
Plantation Rd. SP9: Tid 6G **3**
Plassey Rd. SP9: Tid 4F **3**
(not continuous)
Player Ct. SP6: Fordi 4F **41**
Pointers Way SP4: Ame 5B **14**
Polden Rd. SP1: Sal 4G **29**
Pollen Cl. SP4: Fig 5G **7**
Pollen La. SP4: Fig 5G **7**
Poores Rd. SP4: Dur 5H **9**
Poplar Way SP1: Sal 4G **21**
Portfield Rd. SP5: Bis 5A **26**
Portland Av. SP2: Sal 6D **28**
PORTON 1F **17**

Porton Rd. SP4: Ame 3B 14
Portway
  SP4: Old S, Wint E, Wint G . . .2E 21 & 6A 16
Portway, The SP1: Strat C 5D 20
  SP4: Wint G .4C 16
Portway Bus. Cen. SP4: Old S 2F 21
Potters Way SP1: Lav 2H 29
Pouncette Cl. SP4: Ame 5H 15
Power Rd. SP4: Lark 4B 8
Pownall Rd. SP4: Lark 6E 9
Pretoria Rd. SP11: Fab 2G 5
Primrose Hill SP2: Wilt 5D 18
Primrose La. SP5: Woodf 3F 39
Primrose Pl. SP4: Dur 4G 9
Primrose Rd. SP2: Sal 5A 20
  SP11: Lud 1E 5
Prince Charles Cl. SP11: Lud 1E 5
Prince of Wales Ho. SP11: Lud 1E 5
  (off Andover Rd.)
Princes Cl. SP5: Red 2H 39
Princes Hill SP5: Red 2H 39
Princess Mary Gdns. SP11: Lud 1E 5
Priory Cl. SP2: Wilt 1C 26
  SP5: Alderb 3H 37
Priory Sq. SP2: Sal 3A 42 (2E 29)
Provost Rd. SP4: Bul C 6F 11
Provost St. SP6: Fordi 5F 41
Puddle Slosh La. SP6: Fordi 4D 40
Pullman Dr. SP2: Sal 6H 19
Purvis Cl. SP4: Ame 5C 14

Q

Quadrant SP6: Fordi 6F 41
Quavey Rd. SP5: Red 3H 39
Queen Alexandra Rd. SP2: Sal 1A 28
Queen Mnr. Rd. SP1: Lav, Sal 3H 29
  SP5: Lav 6D 22
Queen Mary Rd. SP2: Sal 6B 20
Queensberry Rd. SP1: Sal 6E 21
  SP4: Ame 4A 14
Queens Cl. SP11: Lud 1E 5
Queens Gdns. SP6: Fordi 4F 41
Queens Rd. SP1: Sal 1C 42 (1F 29)
Queen St. SP1: Sal 3C 42 (2F 29)
  SP2: Wilt 5D 18
Queensway SP4: N'avon 2F 7
Queenswood Ho. SP2: Sal 4A 42 (3E 29)
QUIDHAMPTON .6F 19

R

Race Plain, The SP2: N'ton 6D 26
Race Plain Rd. SP2: N'ton 3E 27
Radcliffe Rd. SP2: Sal 5E 29
Radnor Rd. SP1: Sal 6E 21
Ragan Ct. SP2: Sal 1C 28
Railway Ct. SP2: Sal 2D 28
Raleigh Cres. SP4: Ame 5B 14
Rambridge Cres. SP2: Sal 5H 19
Ramleaze Dr. SP2: Sal 4H 19
Rampart Rd. SP1: Sal 3D 42 (2F 29)
Ramsbury Dr. SP4: Old S 2F 21
Randall's Cft. Rd. SP2: Wilt 1B 26
RATFYN 2A 14
Ratfyn Farm Bungs. SP4: Ame 3A 14
Ratfyn Rd. SP4: Ame 4H 13
Ravenscroft SP2: Sal 6E 29
Rawlence Rd. SP2: Sal 6H 19
  SP2: Wilt 1C 26
Rawlings Ct. SP11: Lud 1E 5
Rawlinson Rd. SP4: Bul C 1F 15
Raymond McEnhill Stadium 1G 21
Reasons Row SP4: Ame 6B 14
Recreation Rd. SP4: Ame 5F 13
  SP4: Dur 4A 10
  SP11: Lud 1E 5
Rectory Cl. SP9: Tid 5F 3
Rectory La. SP5: Alderb 3G 37
Rectory Rd. SP2: Sal 4A 42 (3D 28)
  SP5: Alderb 4F 37
REDBROOK 6G 41
Redbrook Cotts. SP6: Fordi 6G 41
Redford Cl. SP6: Fordi 6H 21
Redford La. SP11: Lud 1D 4
Red La. SP5: Midd W 5G 25
REDLYNCH 2H 39
Redwood Dr. SP4: Ame 6A 14
Redworth M. SP4: Ame 6A 14

Redwood Wlk. SP4: Ame 6A 14
Reeder Cl. SP6: Fordi 5E 41
Reed Wlk. SP4: Dur 5A 10
Richards Way SP2: Sal 4B 28
Richmond Cres. SP9: Tid 5H 3
Richmond Rd. SP2: Sal 1D 28
Ridge, The SP5: Red, Woodf 5G 39
Ridgeway Rd. SP1: Sal 6F 21
Ridgmount SP4: Dur 4H 9
Rifles (Berkshire & Wiltshire) Museum, The
  (The Wardrobe) 5A 42 (3E 29)
Rings, The SP1: Strat C 3C 20
Ringwood Av. SP4: Ame 5A 14
Ringwood Rd. SP6: Fordi 6G 41
Riverbourne Rd. SP1: Sal 3H 29
Riverdale Cl. SP6: Fordi 4F 41
River M. SP6: Fordi 5F 41
Riverside SP1: Sal 2B 42
  SP2: Wilt 6D 18
Riverside Av. SP4: Ame 5F 13
Riverside Cl. SP1: Lav 1H 29
Riverside Pl. SP6: Fordi 5F 41
Riverside Rd. SP1: Lav 2H 29
Riverside Wlk. SP1: Sal 4F 29
River Way SP4: Dur 5A 10
Robbins Ridge SP4: Ame 6A 14
Roberts Rd. SP2: Sal 6B 20
  SP11: Lud 2D 4
Robert Stokes Almshouse SP1: Sal 6C 42
Robin Hill La. SP4: Dur 5A 8
Rocheford Cl. SP5: Midd W 5H 25
Rockbourne Rd. SP6: Roc, San 1A 40
Rockrose Ct. SP11: Lud 2E 5
Rogers Cl. SP2: Quid 6G 19
Rolfes Ct. SP1: Sal 4C 42
Rollestone St. SP1: Sal 3C 42 (2F 29)
Roman Mdw. SP5: Dow 2C 38
Roman Quay SP6: Fordi 5F 41
Roman Rd. SP2: Sal 1B 28
Romer Rd. SP2: Sal 5E 29
Romsey Rd. SP4: Ame 6B 14
Rookery, The SP5: Coombe B 4F 33
Rookwood Gdns. SP6: Fordi 5D 40
Rosemary Cl. SP1: Lav 2H 29
Rosemary La. SP1: Sal 5B 42 (3E 29)
Ross Rd. SP4: Lark 5A 8
Rougemont Cl. SP1: Sal 2D 42 (2F 29)
Round Hill SP6: Fordi 5F 41
Row, The SP5: Red 2G 39
Rowan Cl. SP2: Sal 5H 19
  SP4: Dur 4G 9
Rowbarrow SP2: Sal 6F 29
Rowbarrow Cl. SP2: Sal 6F 29
Rowbarrow La. SP2: Sal 6F 29
Rowbarrow M. SP2: Sal 6F 29
  (off Rowbarrow La.)
Royal Crescent, The SP9: Tid 4G 3
Roy's Cl. SP11: Lud 1E 5
Rushworth Row SP4: Ame 6A 14
Russell Rd. SP2: Sal 1C 28
Russell St. SP2: Wilt 6D 18

S

Saddlers Cl. SP6: Fordi 5F 41
Saddlers Mead SP2: Wilt 6C 18
St Albans Cl. SP1: Sal 4H 21
St Andrews SP1: Lav 1A 30
St Andrew's Cl. SP2: Wilt 1B 26
St Andrews Rd. SP2: Sal 1A 28
  SP9: Tid 5F 3
St Annes Cl. SP4: Ame 4A 14
St Ann Gate 5C 42 (3E 29)
St Ann Pl. SP1: Sal 5C 42 (3F 29)
St Ann's Ct. SP1: Sal 5C 42 (3F 29)
St Ann St. SP1: Sal 5C 42 (3F 29)
St Bedes Cl. SP1: Sal 4H 21
St Birinus Rd. SP5: Woodf 3G 39
St Brendans Cl. SP1: Sal 4G 21
St Christophers Cl. SP1: Sal 4H 21
St Clair Rd. SP2: Sal 4G 21
St Clements M. SP2: Sal 3A 42
St Clements Way SP1: Sal 4G 21
St Davids Cl. SP1: Sal 4H 21
St Edith's Cl. SP2: Wilt 2C 26
St Edmund's Church St. SP1: Sal . .2C 42 (2F 29)
St Edmunds Ga. SP1: Sal 3C 42
St Edwards Mdw. SP4: Wint D 5D 16
Saintes Cl. SP1: Sal 4G 21
St Francis Cres. SP1: Sal 4F 21

St Francis Rd. SP1: Sal 5E 21
St Georges Cl. SP2: Sal 4D 28
  SP9: Tid 6F 3
St George's Cotts. SP6: Hale 6G 39
St Georges Cres. SP6: Fordi 4F 41
St Georges Rd. SP2: Sal 4B 28
  SP6: Fordi 4F 41
  SP9: Tid 5F 3
St Gregory's Av. SP2: Sal 1B 28
St James Cl. SP1: Sal 4H 21
St James St. SP11: Lud 1D 4
St James Way SP4: Dur 4H 9
St John's Cl. SP1: Sal 3H 29
St John's Ct. SP2: Wilt 5C 18
St John's Priory SP2: Wilt 6C 18
St John's Sq. SP1: Sal 6C 18
St John's St. SP1: Sal 5C 42 (3F 29)
St Joseph's Cl. SP1: Sal 4H 21
St Judes Cl. SP1: Sal 5H 21
St Lawrence Cl. SP1: Strat C 4C 20
St Leonard's Cl. SP4: Bul 6B 10
St Lukes Cl. SP1: Sal 4H 21
St Margaret's Cl. SP1: Sal 3G 29
St Mark's Av. SP1: Sal 6F 21
St Mark's Ho. SP1: Sal 1G 29
  (off St Mark's Av.)
St Mark's Rd. SP1: Sal 1C 42 (1F 29)
St Mark's Rdbt. SP1: Sal 1G 29
St Martin's Church St. SP1: Sal . . .5D 42 (3F 29)
St Martin's Ter. SP1: Sal 5D 42
St Mary's Cl. SP2: Wilt 2C 26
St Mary's Ct. SP2: Sal 1D 28
St Mary's Rd. SP2: Sal 4D 28
St Matthews Cl. SP1: Sal 4H 21
St Michaels Av. SP9: Tid 6F 3
St Michael's Cl. SP2: Wilt 2B 26
St Michaels Grn. SP9: Tid 6F 3
St Michael's Rd. SP2: Sal 5A 20
St Michaels Vw. SP9: Tid 4G 3
St Nicholas Cl. SP2: Wilt 2B 26
  SP4: Por 2F 17
  SP11: Lud 1G 5
St Nicholas Hospital (Almshouse)
  SP1: Sal 6B 42 (4E 29)
St Nicholas' Rd. SP1: Sal 6B 42 (4E 29)
St Osmund's Cl. SP1: Sal 4E 21
St Patricks Av. SP9: Tid 6E 3
St Paul's Rd. SP2: Sal 2A 42 (2D 28)
St Paul's Rdbt. SP2: Sal 2D 28
St Peter's Cl. SP2: Wilt 1C 26
St Peters Rd. SP1: Sal 4G 21
St Teresas Cl. SP1: Sal 5G 21
St Thomas's Sq. SP1: Sal 3B 42 (3E 29)
St Thomas Way SP1: Sal 4G 21
St Ursula's Cl. SP1: Sal 5H 21
Salamander Ct. SP9: Tid 6E 3
SALISBURY 4B 42 (3E 29)
Salisbury & South Wilts Golf Course 4G 27
Salisbury & South Wiltshire Mus.
  . . . . .6A 42 (4E 29)
Salisbury & South Wiltshire Sports Club
  . . . . .1A 28
Salisbury Arts Cen. 2C 42 (2F 29)
Salisbury Bus. Pk. SP1: Sal 4H 29
Salisbury Cathedral 5B 42 (3E 29)
Salisbury City FC 1G 21
Salisbury Crematorium SP1: Sal 6G 21
SALISBURY DISTRICT HOSPITAL 2F 35
SALISBURY HOSPICE 2F 35
Salisbury Playhouse 3A 42 (2E 29)
Salisbury Poultry Cross 4B 42
  (off Minster St.)
Salisbury Racecourse 6F 27
Salisbury Rd. SP2: Wilt 6E 19
  SP4: Ame 5H 13
  SP4: Bul 1B 14
  SP4: N'avon 1E 7
  SP5: Coombe B 3F 33
  SP5: Dow 1B 38
  SP6: Bre, Bur, Fordi . . . . . .5G 41 & 6A 38
Salisbury Snooker Club 3G 29
Salisbury Station (Rail) 2D 28
Salisbury St. SP4: Ame 5G 13
  SP6: Fordi 5F 41
Salt La. SP1: Sal 3C 42 (2F 29)
  SP4: Wint G 4E 17
Sandel Pl. SP4: Ame 5B 14
Sandle Copse SP6: Fordi 4B 40
SANDLEHEATH .4A 40
Sandleheath Ind. Est. SP6: San 4B 40
Sandleheath Rd. SP6: Alderh 5A 40

Sandle Mnr. Dr. SP6: Fordi 4C 40
Sandown Pl. SP2: Sal 3A 42
Sandringham Ct. *SP2: Sal* 2D 28
                            (off Gas La.)
Sandringhams, The SP5: Whad 4H 37
Sandy La. SP5: Red 2H 39
Sarum Bus. Pk. SP4: Old S 1G 21
Sarum Cen. SP4: Old S 2F 21
Sarum Cl. SP2: Sal 6C 20
Sassoon Cl. SP2: Sal 6A 20
Saxon Ct. SP9: Tid 4G 3
Saxonhurst SP5: Dow 2D 38
Saxon Leas SP5: Midd W 6G 25
Saxon Mdw. SP5: Dow 2C 38
Saxon Rd. SP2: Sal 5D 28
Scamell's Rd. SP1: Sal 1A 42 (1E 29)
Scholars Cl. SP11: Lud 1E 5
School Dr. SP4: Dur 5H 9
School Hill SP5: Alderb 3E 37
School La. SP1: Sal 2C 42 (2F 29)
  SP4: Ame 4H 13
School Rd. SP4: Dur 4A 10
Scots La. SP1: Sal 3B 42 (1E 29)
Scotts Cl. SP5: Dow 1B 38
Seagrim Rd. SP2: Wilt 1C 26
Senior Dr. SP2: Sal 6F 29
Seth Ward Dr. SP1: Sal 6G 21
Shady Bower SP1: Sal 3G 29
Shady Bower Cl. SP1: Sal 3G 29
Shaftesbury Drove SP2: Sal 6C 28
Shaftesbury Rd. SP2: Wilt 6B 18
Shaftesbury St. SP6: Fordi 5E 41
Shakespeare Rd. SP1: Sal 5D 20
Sharpley Cl. SP6: Fordi 3E 41
Sharratt Av. SP1: Sal 4G 21
Shaston Ct. SP2: Wilt 6C 18
Shaston Drove SP2: N'ton, Wilt 5B 26
  SP5: Coombe B 6B 28
Shears Dr. SP4: Ame 5G 15
Sheen Cl. SP2: Sal 4H 19
Sheepbridge Rd. SP4: Bul C 4F 11
Shelley Dr. SP1: Sal 5D 20
Shepherds Cl. SP5: Coombe B 4G 33
  SP5: Ods 5F 35
Sherbourne Dr. SP4: Old S 1F 21
Sherbourne Ho. SP4: Old S 1F 21
Sherfield SP4: Wint D 5C 16
Shoddesden La. SP11: Gt S, Lud 4F 5
  SP11: Lit S 5H 5
Shortlands SP2: Wilt 6B 18
Short St. SP11: Lud 1E 5
Shrapnel Rd. SP5: Lark 5A 8
Shripple La. SP5: Midd W 6H 25
Shropshire Cl. SP2: Sal 4A 20
SHUTE END 1D 36
Shute End Rd. SP5: Alderb 6C 30
Shutts La. SP5: Coombe B 4G 33
Sidbury Circular Rd. SP9: Tid 4E 3
Sidbury Hill Av. SP9: Tid 3F 3
Sidings, The *SP1: Sal* 3G 29
                      (off Blakey Rd.)
  SP5: Dow 1D 38
Sidney St. SP2: Sal 2D 28
Signal St. SP4: Bul C 1F 15
Silver St. SP1: Sal 4B 42 (3E 29)
  SP2: Wilt 6D 18
  SP5: Alderb 3D 36
Silver Wood SP5: Alderb 2E 37
Silverwood Dr. SP1: Lav 1A 30
Simmance Way SP4: Ame 5A 14
Simonds Rd. SP11: Lud 1D 4
Skew Bri. Rd. SP2: Sal 1B 28
Skew Rd. SP2: Sal 6H 19
Slab La. SP5: Dow, Woodf 2D 38
Slate Way SP5: Pit 6B 24
Sleepers, The *SP1: Sal* 3G 29
                    (off Tollgate Rd.)
Sling Cotts. SP4: Bul C 4F 11
Sling Rd. SP4: Bul C 5F 11
Smeaton Rd. SP2: Sal 2C 28
Smithfield St. SP4: Ame 5H 13
Solar Way SP4: Ame 4D 14
Solstice Pk. SP4: Ame 4C 14
Solstice Pk. Av. SP4: Ame 4B 14
Solstice Ri. SP4: Ame 5H 13
  SP4: Dur 5A 10
Somerset Rd. SP1: Sal 6F 21
Somme Rd. SP11: Per D 2B 4
Southampton Rd. SP1: Sal 6D 42 (4G 29)
  SP5: Alderb, Whad 2E 37
  SP5: Pet, Sal 4G 29
  SP6: Fordi, God .5G 41

South Bank SP2: N'ton 3E 27
Southbank Ho. *SP1: Sal* 2G 29
                    (off Elm Gro.)
Southbourne Cl. SP4: Por 1F 17
Southbourne Way SP4: Por 1F 17
SOUTH CHARFORD 6A 38
Sth. Charford Drove SP6: Bre 6A 38
South La. SP5: Dow 2B 38
South Mill Cl. SP4: Ame 6H 13
Southmill Hill SP4: Ame 6H 13
South Mill Rd. SP4: Ame 5H 13
Southside SP4: Old S 1H 21
South St. SP2: Sal 3A 42 (2D 28)
  SP2: Wilt 2C 26
SOUTH TIDWORTH 6G 3
Southwark Cl. SP9: Tid 5H 3
Southway SP5: Alderb 3G 37
Sovereign Cl. SP2: Quid 6G 19
Sovereign Ct. *SP2: Sal* 2D 28
            (off Sth. Western Rd.)
Spiders Island SP5: Whad 3H 37
Spinners Ct. SP1: Sal 3C 42 (2F 29)
Spinney Rd. SP11: Lud 1D 4
Spire Vw. SP2: Sal 2A 42 (2D 28)
  SP4: Ford 2B 22
Spire Vw. Pk. SP4: Gom 3F 17
Spitfire Rd. SP4: Old S 1H 21
Spray Leaze SP11: Lud 1G 5
Spring Ct. *SP2: Sal* 2D 28
                  (off Windsor Rd.)
Springfield Cres. SP5: Woodf 4G 39
Springfields SP11: Lud 1D 4
Square, The SP2: Sal 4A 42 (3E 29)
Squarey Cl. SP5: Dow 3C 38
Stable Cl. SP11: Lud 2D 4
Stanley Ct. SP2: Sal 3C 28
Stanley Lit. Rd. SP2: Sal 6H 19
Station App. SP11: Lud 1E 5
Station Rd. SP6: Fordi 4C 40
  SP9: Tid 6G 3
Station Ter. *SP2: Sal* 2D 28
                  (off Windsor Rd.)
Steadings, The SP4: Ford 3H 21
Stephen Martin Gdns.
  SP6: Fordi 4E 41
Stephens Cl. SP2: Sal 4C 28
Stephenson Rd. SP2: Sal 3C 28
Stockbarrow Rd. SP4: Ame 5A 14
Stockport Rd. SP4: Ame 6H 15
Stocks Bri. La. SP5: Coombe B 4G 33
Stockwood Cl. SP1: Sal 6G 21
Stockwood Cl. SP5: Midd W 6G 25
Stonehenge Golf Cen. 5E 9
Stonehenge Rd. SP4: Ame 4F 13
  SP4: Dur 5G 9
Stonehenge Vis. Cen. 6B 12
Stonehenge Wlk. SP4: Ame 4G 13
Stonehenge (World Heritage Site) 3A 12
Stonemasons Yd. SP1: Sal 5D 42 (3G 29)
Stoney Cross SP11: Lud 1E 5
Strangways SP5: Lark 1D 12
Stratford Rd. SP1: Sal, Strat C 4C 20
STRATFORD SUB CASTLE 4C 20
STRATFORD TONY 4C 32
Stratford Tony Rd. SP5: Coombe B 3E 33
Street, The SP5: W Win 4F 25
Stroud Pl. *SP1: Sal* 2G 29
                  (off Manor Rd.)
STUCKTON 6H 41
Stuckton Rd. SP6: Fordi, Stru 5G 41
Studio Theatre
  Salisbury 1E 29
Suffolk Rd. SP2: Sal 5C 28
Summerlock App. SP2: Sal 3A 42 (2E 29)
Summerlug SP4: Wint E 6C 16
Sunnyhill Rd. SP4: Ame 5E 21
Sun Rise Way SP4: Ame 4B 14
Sussex Rd. SP2: Sal 5C 28
Suvla La. SP4: Bul C 6E 11
Swallow Cl. SP9: Tid 5G 3
Swallowmead SP2: Sal 6E 29
Swan Cl. SP2: Sal 5E 29
  SP4: Dur 5A 10
Swattons Cl. SP4: Bul 6C 10
Swayne Rd. SP2: Wilt 2C 26
Swayne's Cl. SP1: Sal 1C 42 (1F 29)
Swiftdown SP2: Sal 6E 29
Swindon Rd. *SP9: Tid* 4G 3
                  (off Wylye Rd.)

Sycamore Cl. SP9: Tid 5H 3
Sycamore Cl. SP6: Fordi 5F 41
Sycamore Dr. SP1: Sal 4G 21
Syringa Ct. SP2: Sal 2B 28

T

Talbot Cl. SP1: Sal 5G 21
Tanners Cl. SP4: Wint E 6C 16
Tanners Fld. SP4: Ame 5B 14
Tanners La. SP4: Wint E 6C 16
  SP6: San 4A 40
Teasel Cl. SP11: Lud 2E 5
Telford Rd. SP2: Sal 3C 28
Tempest Rd. SP4: Ame 5B 14
Tethering Drove SP6: Hale 6G 39
Thaxted SP1: Sal 1D 42 (1F 29)
The . . . .
  Names prefixed with 'The' for example
  'The Alders' are indexed under the
  main name such as 'Alders, The'
Thistlebarrow Rd. SP1: Sal 5E 21
Thompson Cl. SP2: Sal 6D 28
Thorne Cl. SP5: Coombe B 4F 33
Thorne Rd. SP4: N'avon 1E 7
Thorneydown Rd. SP4: Gom, Wint G 4E 17
  SP5: Firs 4E 17
Thornton Cres. SP2: Wilt 5F 19
Three Colts La. SP5: Bis 4A 32
Three Cuppes La. SP1: Sal 3C 42
Throgmorton Hall SP4: Old S 1H 21
Thurlow Cl. SP4: Ame 5C 14
TIDWORTH 5G 3
TIDWORTH CAMP 6E 3
Tidworth Garrison Golf Course 6B 2
Tidworth Leisure Cen. 5G 3
Tidworth Rd. SP4: All, Idm, Por 1E 17
  SP4: Bul C 5F 11
  SP11: Lud 2B 4
Timbermill Ct. SP6: Fordi 6F 41
TINKERS CROSS 2E 11
Tinneys Cl. SP5: Woodf 5G 39
Tintern Ct. SP1: Sal 6D 42 (4F 29)
Tollgate Cl. SP4: Ame 3G 13
Tollgate Rd. SP1: Sal 5D 42 (3G 29)
Tombs Rd. SP4: Lark 6E 9
Tourist Info. Cen.
  Fordingbridge 5F 41
  Salisbury 4B 42 (2E 29)
Tournament Rd. SP2: Sal 6A 20
Towell Rd. SP4: Lark 6F 9
Tower M. SP1: Sal 1F 29
Town Path SP2: Sal 4C 28
                  (not continuous)
Townsend SP5: Pit 5C 24
Trafalgar Sq. SP4: Wint G 5E 17
Trenchard Av. SP4: Wint G 5E 17
Trinity St. SP1: Sal 5C 42 (3F 29)
Trinity Vw. Rd. SP9: Tid 5F 3
Tryhorn Dr. SP1: Sal 4G 21
Tucker Cl. SP4: Ame 6A 14
Tunnel Hill SP5: Alderb 3D 36
Turner Cl. SP2: Sal 4C 28
Twineham Gdns. SP5: Alderb 3G 37
Twynham Cl. SP5: Dow 3C 38
Tylers Cl. SP2: Sal 4B 28
Tyrone Av. SP4: Bul C 5E 11
Tytherley Rd. SP5: Midd W 6H 25

U

UGFORD 6A 18
Underwood Dr. SP4: Ame 6B 14
Upnor Cl. SP11: Per D 4C 4
UPPER BURGATE 1G 41
Upper Folly SP2: Wilt 2B 26
Upper St. SP2: Sal 4B 28
Urchfont Ho. *SP9: Tid* 5H 3
                  (off Bourne Rd.)

V

Valentine Ct. SP2: Sal 1A 42
Vale Rd. SP5: Woodf 3G 39
Valley, The SP2: Sal 4A 20
Valley Cl. SP5: Woodf 3G 39
Vanessa Av. SP1: Lav 2H 29
Ventry, The SP1: Sal 1D 42 (1F 29)

Ventry Cl. SP1: Sal 1D **42** (1F **29**)
Verney Cl. SP4: Ame 5B **14**
Vernon Cl. SP4: Ame 5C **14**
Verona Rd. SP1: Sal 5D **20**
Vicarage Gdns. SP4: N'avon 2F **7**
Vicarage Pk. SP5: Mor V 3G **39**
Victoria Cl. SP2: Wilt 6C **18**
Victoria Ct. SP1: Sal 6E **21**
Victoria Flats SP2: Wilt 5C **18**
Victoria Gdns. SP6: Fordi 5D **40**
Victoria Rd. SP1: Sal 6E **21**
   SP2: Wilt 6B **18**
   SP6: Fordi 5D **40**
Viking Way SP1: Sal 6F **29**
Vimoutiers Ct. SP6: Fordi 5E **41**
Violet Ct. SP11: Lud 1D **4**
Virginia Cl. SP4: Ame 5B **14**
Vockins Cl. SP9: Tid 3F **3**

W

Wain-a-Long Rd. SP1: Sal 2G **29**
Wains Way SP4: N'avon 2F **7**
Waleran Cl. SP5: Alderb 3G **37**
Walnut Cl. SP4: N'avon 1E **7**
Wardrobe, The (The Rifles Mus.)
   . . . . .5A **42** (3E **29**)
Warminster Ho. SP9: Tid 4G **3**
   (off Wylye Rd.)
Warminster Rd. SP2: Wilt 4D **18**
Warren, The SP11: Per D 5C **4**
Warwick Cl. SP1: Sal 6D **20**
Washern Cl. SP2: Wilt 2C **26**
Wason Rd. SP4: Lark 6B **8**
Water Ditchampton SP2: Wilt 5C **18**
Watergate La. SP4: Bul 1H **13**
Water La. SP2: Sal 3A **42** (2D **28**)
Waterloo Rd. SP1: Sal 4G **29**
Waterside SP5: Dow 2D **38**
Watersmeet Rd. SP2: Sal 5E **29**
Waters Rd. SP1: Sal 5E **21**
Water St. SP4: Bul 6B **10**
Watson Rd. SP4: Lark 5B **8**
Watt Rd. SP2: Sal 3B **28**
Wavell Rd. SP2: Sal 5E **29**
   SP9: Tid 3E **3**
Waverley Cl. SP4: Bul C 6F **11**
   SP6: Fordi 3F **41**
Waverley Rd. SP6: Fordi 3F **41**
Weavers Cl. SP5: Midd W 6G **25**
Weeke Cl. SP5: Dow 2A **38**
Wellington Academy Health & Fitness Club, The
   . . . . .2B **4**
Wellington M. SP1: Sal 3G **29**
   (off Waterloo Rd.)
Wellington Rd. SP4: Bul C 5G **11**
Wellington Way SP2: Sal 6B **20**
Wells Cl. SP4: Lark 6F **9**
Wells Rd. SP4: Lark 1E **13**
Wellworthy Dr. SP2: Sal 4B **28**
Wessex Rd. SP1: Sal 2G **29**
   SP2: Sal .2B **26**
WEST AMESBURY 5E **13**
Westbourne Cl. SP1: Sal 3G **29**
West End Rd. SP2: Sal 1C **28**

Western Way SP2: Sal 6H **19**
Westfield Cl. SP1: Lav 1A **30**
   SP4: Dur .5G **9**
WEST GOMELDON 2E **17**
Westgrove SP6: Fordi 5E **41**
Westland Cl. SP4: Ame 5B **14**
West Mills Rd. SP6: Fordi 5E **41**
Westminster Rd. SP2: Sal 1D **28**
Weston La. SP5: Midd W . . . . .4G **25** & 6G **25**
Westside Cl. SP4: Old S 1G **21**
West St. SP2: Sal 3A **42** (2D **28**)
   SP2: Wilt 6C **18**
   SP6: Fordi 5E **41**
West Wlk. SP1: Sal 5A **42** (3E **29**)
West Wick SP5: Dow 1A **38**
WEST WINTERSLOW 4G **25**
WESTWOOD 4H **19**
Westwood Ho. SP2: Sal 1C **28**
Westwood Rd. SP2: Sal 5H **19**
Wexland Av. SP4: N'avon 3D **6**
WHADDON 4H **37**
Whaddon Bus. Pk. SP5: Whad 4H **37**
Wheelwright M. SP5: Dow 2A **38**
Whelan Way SP4: Ame 5B **14**
   (off Butterfield Dr.)
Whinyates Rd. SP4: Lark 5B **8**
Whitbred Rd. SP2: Sal 4A **20**
Whitchers Mdw. SP5: Alderb 1F **37**
Whitebridge Rd. SP1: Sal 2H **29**
Whitefriars Rd. SP1: Sal 6C **42** (4F **29**)
Whitehill SP5: Pit 6C **24**
Whiteshoot SP5: Red 5H **39**
Whiteshoot Hill SP5: Red, Woodf 5H **39**
White Way SP5: Pit 6C **24**
Whitmarsh Cl. SP4: N'avon 1F **7**
Whitsbury Rd. SP5: Ods 4F **35**
   SP6: Fordi 1D **40**
Whittle Rd. SP2: Sal 2B **28**
WICK 1B **38**
Wick La. SP5: Dow 1A **38**
Wilcot Cl. SP4: Ame 6B **14**
Wiley Ter. SP2: Wilt 5D **18**
William Cl. SP1: Lav 2H **29**
Williamson Cl. SP11: Lud 1D **4**
Willoughby Rd. SP4: Lark 6A **8**
Willow Av. SP6: Fordi 4E **41**
Willow Cl. SP1: Lav 1H **29**
Willow Dr. SP4: Dur 4G **9**
Willowmead Cl. SP5: Coombe B 4F **33**
Wilman Way SP2: Sal 6D **28**
Wilson Ct. SP6: Fordi 5F **41**
Wilson Rd. SP4: Lark 6B **8**
WILTON 6D **18**
Wilton (Park & Ride) 4E **19**
Wilton House 1D **26**
Wilton Ct. 1E **27**
Wilton Rd. SP2: Quid, Sal 6F **19**
Wilton Shop. Village, The SP2: Wilt 6D **18**
Wiltshire Cl. SP4: Bul 6D **10**
Wiltshire Rd. SP2: Sal 4C **28**
Wiltshire Ter. SP2: Sal 4C **28**
Winchester Cl. SP4: Ame 6B **14**
Winchester St. SP1: Sal 3C **42** (2F **29**)
Winding Way SP2: Sal 6H **19**
Windlesham Rd. SP1: Sal 5F **21**
Windmill Cl. SP5: Alderb 3G **37**

Windmill La. SP4: Gom 3D **16**
Windsor M. SP4: Dur 4H **9**
Windsor Rd. SP2: Sal 2D **28**
   SP4: Dur .4H **9**
Windsor St. SP2: Sal 2D **28**
Windwhistle Way SP5: Alderb 3H **37**
Wing Rd. SP4: Bul C 6E **11**
WINTERBOURNE DAUNTSEY 5D **16**
WINTERBOURNE EARLS 1B **22**
WINTERBOURNE GUNNER 4E **17**
Winterslow Rd. SP4: Por 1F **17**
Winton Cl. SP9: Tid 6G **3**
Wishford Rd. SP2: Wilt 4C **18**
WITHERINGTON 6E **37**
Witherington Rd.
   SP5: Alderb, Dow 3D **36**
Wittenham Vw. SP4: Ame 6A **14**
Witt Rd. SP5: Midd W 6H **25**
Wolferstan Dr. SP1: Sal 4H **21**
Woodbury Gdns. SP2: Sal 5F **29**
Woodbury Ho. SP2: Sal 6F **29**
Woodbury La. SP2: Sal 6F **29**
Woodbury Ri. SP2: Sal 6F **29**
Woodbury Yd. SP2: Sal 6F **29**
WOODFALLS 4G **39**
Woodhenge 1F **13**
Woodland Dr. SP5: Midd W 2H **25**
Woodland Way SP1: Lav 1A **30**
Woodlea Grange SP5: Alderb 2G **37**
Wood Pk. SP11: Lud 1F **5**
Wood Rd. SP4: Lark 6E **9**
Woodside Rd. SP2: Sal 6A **20**
Woodstock Rd. SP1: Sal 1C **42** (1F **29**)
Woodvill Rd. SP1: Sal 5H **21**
Wordsworth Rd. SP1: Sal 1C **42** (1F **29**)
Wouldham Cl. SP11: Per D 4C **4**
Wrenscroft SP2: Sal 6E **29**
Wyld Ho. SP1: Sal 3G **29**
Wylye Cl. SP2: Quid 1F **27**
Wylye Lodge SP2: Wilt 6D **18**
Wylye Rd. SP9: Tid 5G **3**
Wyndham Centre, The
   SP1: Sal .4H **29**
WYNDHAM PARK 1D **42** (2F **29**)
Wyndham Pk. SP1: Sal 1C **42** (1F **29**)
Wyndham Rd. SP1: Sal 1B **42** (1E **29**)
Wyndham Ter. SP1: Sal 1C **42** (1F **29**)
Wyvern Rd. SP4: Bul C 1F **15**

Y

Yarmley La. SP5: Midd W 3H **25**
Yew Tree Cl. SP5: Midd W 3H **25**
Yewtree Ct. SP4: Dur 5A **10**
Yew Tree Ct. SP6: Fordi 5E **41**
York Rd. SP2: Sal 2A **42** (2D **28**)
Youngs Paddock SP5: Midd W 6G **25**

Z

Zouch Av. SP9: Tid 4F **3**
Zouch Cl. SP9: Tid 4F **3**
Zouch Farm Rd. SP9: Tid 4F **3**
Zouch Mkt. SP9: Tid 4F **3**

SAFETY CAMERA INFORMATION

PocketGPSWorld.com's CamerAlert is a self-contained speed and red light camera warning system for SatNavs and Android or Apple iOS smartphones/tablets. Visit www.cameralert.co.uk to download.

Safety camera locations are publicised by the Safer Roads Partnership which operates them in order to encourage drivers to comply with speed limits at these sites. It is the driver's absolute responsibility to be aware of and to adhere to speed limits at all times.

By showing this safety camera information it is the intention of Geographers' A-Z Map Company Ltd., to encourage safe driving and greater awareness of speed limits and vehicle speed. Data accurate at time of printing.